NETTLES

Other Books by Vénus Khoury-Ghata

POETRY

La Voix des arbres
Quelle est la nuit parmi les nuits
Compassion des pierres
Elle dit
Anthologie personnelle
Ils
Fables pour un peuple d'argile
Leçon d'arithmétique au grillon
Monologue du mort
Un faux pas du soleil
Qui parle au nom du jasmin
Les Ombres et leurs cris
Au sud du silence
Terres stagnantes

FICTION

La maison aux orties
Sept pierres pour la femme adultère
Zarife la folle et autres nouvelles
Le Moine, l'ottoman et la femme du grand argentier
Une Maison au bord des larmes
Privilège des morts
La Maestra
Les Fiancées du cap Tenès
Les Fugues d'Olympia
La Maîtresse du notable
Bayarmine
Mortemaison
Les Morts n'ont pas d'ombre
Vacarme pour une lune morte
Alma cousue main
Le Fils empaillé
Dialogue à propos d'un Christ ou d'un acrobate
Les Inadaptés

Other Books by Marilyn Hacker

POETRY

Essays on Departure: New and Selected Poems
Desesperanto
First Cities: Collected Early Poems
Squares and Courtyards
Winter Numbers
Selected Poems 1965–1990
Going Back to the River
Love, Death, and the Changing of the Seasons
Assumptions
Taking Notice
Separations
Presentation Piece

TRANSLATIONS

Charlestown Blues by Guy Goffette
A House at the Edge of Tears by Vénus Khoury-Ghata
She Says by Vénus Khoury-Ghata
Here There Was Once a Country by Vénus Khoury-Ghata
A Long-Gone Sun by Claire Malroux
Edge by Claire Malroux
Birds and Bison by Claire Malroux

NETTLES

POEMS BY

Vénus Khoury-Ghata

Translated from the French by Marilyn Hacker

Graywolf Press

SAINT PAUL, MINNESOTA

Publication of this volume is made possible in part by a grant provided by the Minnesota State Arts Board, through an appropriation by the Minnesota State Legislature; a grant from the Wells Fargo Foundation Minnesota; and a grant from the National Endowment for the Arts, which believes that a great nation deserves great art. Significant support has also been provided by the Bush Foundation; Target; the McKnight Foundation; and other generous contributions from foundations, corporations, and individuals. To these organizations and individuals we offer our heartfelt thanks.

MINNESOTA
STATE ARTS BOARD

NATIONAL
ENDOWMENT
FOR THE ARTS

TARGET.

A Lannan Translation Selection
Funding the translation and publication of exceptional literary works

Nettles contains poems originally published in French in *Quelle est la nuit parmi les nuits*, published by Mercure de France, 2004.

Grateful acknowledgment is given to the editors of the journals in which some of these translations first appeared: *Artful Dodge, Banipal: A Journal of Modern Arab Literature* (UK), *Chelsea, Circumference: Poetry in Translation, Columbia, Crazyhorse, Field, Modern Poetry in Translation* (UK), *PN Review* (UK), *Poetry London* (UK), *Poetry Northwest, Washington Square*, and *WordsWithoutBorders*.

Published by Graywolf Press
2402 University Avenue, Suite 203
Saint Paul, Minnesota 55114
All rights reserved.

www.graywolfpress.org

Published in the United States of America

ISBN 978-1-55597-487-9

2 4 6 8 9 7 5 3 1
First Graywolf Printing, 2008

Library of Congress Control Number: 2007924772

Cover design: Kyle G. Hunter
Cover art: © Veer

CONTENTS

TRANSLATOR'S PREFACE

Vénus Khoury-Ghata was born in Lebanon in December 1937. She has lived in France since 1972. Not a child of the intelligentsia or the diplomatic world like many literary émigrés, she was born to a Maronite Christian family, one of four children of a policeman/interpreter and a housewife she has described as "illiterate in two languages." It was the poet's younger brother who first aspired to a literary career; it was also her brother who was the tyrannical father's scapegoat, who turned to drugs in his teens and was paternally immured in a rudimentary mental hospital. This marking story was recounted lyrically by Khoury-Ghata in *Une maison au bord des larmes* (published by Graywolf Press as *A House at the Edge of Tears* in 2005)—one of only two of her nineteen novels that eschews fictional invention for autobiographical elaboration. This novel shares the counterpoint present in all of Khoury-Ghata's poetry, between the immediate lyric or narrative and the backdrop of contemporary history—the history of war-torn Lebanon. In the construction of the poet's personal myth of origins, it was the silencing of the gifted, vulnerable brother which gave his sister access to the written word. (In the same year as Khoury-Ghata published *Une maison au bord des larmes*, her sister, the journalist May Ménassa, who stayed in Lebanon and writes in Arabic, published a novel on the same subject. Neither sister knew of the other's project before the books appeared.)

As well as the nineteen novels, Khoury-Ghata is the author of sixteen collections of poetry. *Nettles* contains poems from *Quelle est la nuit parmi les nuits* (Mercure de France, 2004), as well as a new sequence, "The Darkened Ones" ("Les Obscurcis"), written during the war waged on Lebanon by the Israeli army in 2006. *Quelle est la*

< vii >

nuit parmi les nuits was followed by the publication of *La maison aux orties (The House of Nettles)*, a hybrid book described as a novel in the French press, in which Khoury-Ghata describes her arrival in France, her ongoing dialogue with her mother, at once a Fate and a Muse, before and after the latter's demise, her second marriage to physician and medical researcher Jean Ghata, his death, and the death of her brother Victor. *La maison aux orties* is not really a "novel," but neither is it a "memoir" in the Anglophone sense. Reality and invention interpenetrate, time collapses; although the protagonist is clearly the author herself, one cannot pin down the events; certain characters are amalgams, hybrids, or pure invention; and "obvious" fantasy (the protagonist's ongoing rendezvous in cafés with her dead husband, for example) is present as a condiment and a challenge to the reader's attention. How much of the story is to be read as allegorically as those meetings? And yet, this idiosyncratic book, as well as *A House at the Edge of Tears,* can also be seen as an example of the French genre of "autofiction," widely practiced since the 1970s and 1980s by, among others, Patrick Modiano and Hervé Guibert, more recently by Leïla Sebbar and Nina Bouraoui, related to the work of Marguerite Duras and Hélène Cixous, perhaps originating with Proust: books in which the narrator ("the Narrator") can be identified with the author, but where this identification is often used to lead the reader into the puzzles and multiple possibilities of fictional invention, often into a consideration of the nature of fiction itself.

Lyric poetry in English since the Romantics at least also often depends upon a "fiction of the self" which is as much a narrative device promoting immediacy of identification as it is a response to any "confessional" impulse. This trope is notably absent from much of contemporary French (and even Francophone) poetry, as widespread as it is in fiction. Khoury-Ghata's exuberant use of narrative in poetry—sometimes a mythos of the self, but more often narrative in all its inventive bravura—has been an affirmative return to poetry's tale-telling sources, as strong in French as anywhere, while her surrealist, or magic realist, imagery honors the verbal shapeshifting familiar to readers of poetry in, or translated from, Arabic. (Khoury-Ghata is herself an active translator of contemporary

< viii >

Arabic poetry into French.) "The Sailors without a Ship" and especially "The Cherry Tree's Journey" evolve like folktales, the former in a tragic register, the latter with a pungent humor (but the more somber poem is not devoid of humor, nor the ludic one of tragedy).

This collection's central sequence, "Nettles," is a lyric-narrative variation on and continuation of the themes established in the writer's two "autofictional" novels, beginning with the characters' insurgency on the writer's imagination. Here is the industrious, semiliterate mother-muse, the mountain village in North Lebanon cut off from the world by snow and wolves in winter, the polyglot autodidact schoolmaster, the violent father, the young sisters witnessing their brother's humiliation. But there is also the shadow of the Palestinian diaspora in Lebanon, and of a different kind of fratricidal violence:

> They arrived every night of every year
> their trees on leashes
> their children planted at the foot of their olive trees
> in her dark cupboard my mother counted their steps
> counted the wing-casings of their rustling bodies
> my mother sympathized . . .

As she oscillates between French and Arabic, poetry and fiction, Khoury-Ghata moves with equal fluidity, in her poems especially, between life and death. Death becomes another mode of life, an ironic one carried on six feet below our surfaces, where the dead, according to the poet's own mythology, and not unlike Homeric shades, "nourish themselves on the smell of our bread, drink the steam rising from our water, live on our noises." Death itself has a double register: as experienced on a personal level, with the deaths of husband, mother, brother, but with the collective specter of 200,000 people dead in Lebanon during the war that marked the poet's youth serving as a chorus in the intimate tragedy—a tragedy echoed in the Israeli invasion of 2006, which claimed more than 1,000 mostly civilian victims.

An idiosyncratic (often humorous or defiant) fascination with

< ix >

death is a cornerstone of Khoury-Ghata's work, making its way into several titles. This began for her "in 1975 with the unbearable images of Lebanon drowned in its own blood. Cadavers were laid out on wooden planks to be shoved into ditches for common burial with the same movement as a baker putting bread into the oven." Death: daily bread for the Lebanese. "I felt guilty about transforming the dead into words, lining them up like lead soldiers on my pages, but I was incapable of turning to another subject. Five years later, this collective death gave way to an individual death, that of my husband, the father of my daughter. Death which I'd picked up and examined barehanded blew up in my face. . . ."

In this new collection, the verbal membrane separating life and death is often permeable. In the sequence with the somber title "Interments," a series of more and more fantastical funerals becomes a chronicle of celebrations:

> A pebble in her hand expresses her grief
> she throws it over her shoulder
> picks up another
> light as the dead man's soul
> smooth as the knees of a little girl on a swing
>
> tomorrow
> earth will open up for a burial
> its emptiness filled by pebbles from a neighboring field
> shared mourning will be like a holiday

But the meditation on death also celebrates the seasonal vicissitudes of life in a Lebanese village, the fabled permutations of the moon, and the relationship of a woman protagonist, not quite sure where she stands between the world of the living and that of the dead, with the useful and omnipresent book she reads—and writes:

> It's in her book that she gathers stones to chase away the foxes
> she hangs her hammock between two lines
> the turned pages flap like laundry on a line

< x >

her finger placed on a word immobilizes a crowd and causes a
    traffic jam in the air
she has something to dream on
but not to live on
in her hands every page becomes a kite

Are the plural speakers in "The Darkened Ones," written during the
2006 war, the dead once more, or the displaced, refugees fleeing
their calcinated villages, or their no longer habitable city blocks?
Are they Lebanese of past generations, "welcoming" newcomers to
an overdetermined warscape? The poet has not written a text to be
deciphered: it establishes its own dramatic parameters, with a cho-
rus of women wringing out laundry providing commentary while
their equestrian daughters escape to live another way.

their daughters who ride the mountain bareback smell the
    heavy stones and storms rolling on the slope
books, they say, are the children of sorrow
the peelings of peelings of the forest
it's better to decipher the sweat on the loins' stretched
    drum-skin
and let a red mare's galloping resonate between your thighs

Vénus Khoury-Ghata's poetic persona, is at once the young woman
riding away, the perennial washerwoman's chorus commenting
and aggrandizing the quotidian, the perennial mourner, and, above
all, as is the writer herself, the woman recreating the world in her
book.

Marilyn Hacker
Paris, 2007

< xi >

NETTLES

VARIATIONS AUTOUR D'UN CERISIER

< 2 >

THE CHERRY TREE'S JOURNEY

< 3 >

Le cerisier ce matin nous fit ses adieux
Il partait pour l'Amérique

à quoi attacherons-nous l'âne demanda la mère
à l'ombre de son tronc répondit le père

Nina qui touillait la neige pour le souper
ajouta trois grains de cumin
au diable l'avarice

———

L'ombre se consume d'amour pour l'arbre absent
midi l'étrécit tache de douleur sous son pied
la terre est opaque de chagrins retenus
où prennent source les larmes?

———

La pluie n'est plus la même depuis la mort du petit frère
dit la mère
jadis elle sortait des volets
laissant le ciel à la neige qui fondait d'étonnement

———

À quoi sert la neige?
à effacer la terre pour la réécrire correctement

———

Le soleil était épineux lorsque la mère planta l'enfant dans la terre
    de retour chez elle
elle démantela la maison
lava les murs dans le fleuve comme elle le fait du linge
les sept cailloux lancés contre le ciel lui revinrent enrobés de
    leur bruit
Un caillou sur la langue du vent médisant
quatre cailloux pour fixer le toit de la réserve
appuyé sur sa bêche
le jardinier est aussi seul que l'arbre qui le regarde

———

< 4 >

The cherry tree said its farewells to us this morning
It's leaving for America

where can we tie up the donkey now, asked the mother
to the shadow of its trunk, the father answered

Nina, who was stirring up snow for supper
added three grains of cumin
stinginess be damned

––––

The shadow is wasting away with love for the absent tree
noon shrinks it to a dark stain underfoot
the earth is opaque with untold sorrows
from what source do these tears spring?

––––

The rain isn't the same since little brother died
says the mother
it used to come out of the shutters
leaving the sky to the snow which melted in astonishment

––––

What use is the snow?
it erases the earth to rewrite it correctly

––––

The sun was thorny when the mother planted the child in the
	earth back at home
she dismantled the house
washed its walls in the river the way she did laundry
the seven pebbles hurled against the sky came back to her coated in
	their noise
A pebble on the tongue of the malicious wind
four pebbles to hold down the roof of the garden shed
leaning on his spade
the gardener is as solitary as the tree which looks at him

––––

< 5 >

Les fleuves qui marchent en ligne droite ne retiennent aucun caillou
Nina en a ramassé trois de la même couleur
quel temps fait-il à la source? leur a-t-elle demandé

————

L'épicéa prépare un mélange de six herbes pour
les mères qui touillent le potage en cercles clos
les enfants morts n'ont qu'à se mettre à table
les mains transies feront la vaisselle
éteindront les lumières
puis claqueront la porte derrière eux dans un froissement d'ailes

————

La mère range les billes par ordre de taille et de tristesse
l'enfant jouera quand il sera moins mort
quand l'herbe qui a poussé sur son lit sera moins blanche
après l'horizon il y a un autre horizon dit-elle en se hissant jusqu'à
    la lucarne
et cette odeur laiteuse de vagues qui applaudissent des deux mains
lorsqu'un petit noyé remonte à la surface
dans sa paume un galet

————

L'ombre du soleil sur l'allée présage oubli et consolation
le père dessine son contour avec un bâton
qu'il plante au milieu du cercle

————

Grand-père récapitule son rêve à l'envers pour
retrouver ses lunettes égarées dans son sommeil
il dit:
fermer les yeux ne change en rien ce qui se passe dans le noir
les vieilles maisons trébuchent dans l'obscurité

————

Nous plions ton ombre le soir écrit le père à Cerisier
nous la rangeons près de la chatte qui a mis bas
six chatons couleur de suie

< 6 >

Rivers which flow in a straight line gather no pebbles
Nina picked up three that were all the same color
What's the weather like at the source? she asked them

———

The spruce tree prepares a mixture of six herbs
for mothers who stir soup in closed circles
dead children have only to come and sit at the table
cold-pierced hands will do the dishes
turn out the lights
then slam the door behind them with a rustling of wings

———

The mother arranges the marbles by size and sadness
the child will play with them when he's less dead
when the grass which grew on his bed is less white
beyond the horizon there's another horizon she says pulling herself
    up to the skylight
and that milky odor of waves which clap with both hands
when a little drowned child comes up to the surface
with a pebble on his palm

———

The sun's shadow on the path presages forgetfulness and consolation
the father draws its outline with a stick
which he plants in the middle of the circle

———

Grandfather goes over his dream backwards
to find his glasses which strayed in his sleep
he says:
closing your eyes doesn't change what happens in the darkness
old houses stagger in the night

———

We fold up your shadow in the evening, writes the father to Cherry Tree
we put it away near the cat who's had a litter
six soot-colored kittens

< 7 >

que décolorera la neige
grand-père a retrouvé ses lunettes dans le poulailler

———

Cerisier a fait fortune en Amérique
sa lettre pèse son poids d'abondance et de prospérité
il épousera une riche Cerisière dit le chat qui plume une caille sur
le seuil

———

Les hommes d'Amérique dorment debout comme les crayons
comme les chevaux
vus de nuit on les prendrait pour des étincelles
des chats les attendent derrière les portes
ils doivent les nourrir et arroser le basilic
j'aurais dû emporter mon ombre avec moi

———

Il pleut sur l'hiver d'Amérique
les moineaux mangent mes noyaux
et jettent la chair par-dessus leurs épaules
je suis seul à droite
seul à gauche
pourquoi n'ai-je pas emporté mon ombre?

———

Dessine ta peur m'a demandé le vent
j'ai dessiné une invasion d'herbes silencieuses
que dessine-t-on dans les pays qui n'ont pas de minaret?
s'interroge un grenadier venu à pied d'Anatolie

———

Les hommes d'Amérique taillent leurs cyprès comme des crayons
écrivent leurs enfants au nord
leurs fenêtres au sud
dessinent Dieu de droite à gauche comme le désert
ventre creux comme l'olivier

< 8 >

who'll be bleached by the snow
grandfather found his glasses in the chicken house

——

Cherry Tree has made his fortune in America
his letter is weighed down with abundance and prosperity
he will marry a rich lady Cherry Tree, says the cat who's plucking
    a quail on the doorstep

——

People in America sleep standing up like pencils
like horses
seen at night one would take them for splinters
cats wait for them behind their doors
they have to feed them and water the basil
I should have brought my shadow with me

——

It's raining on the winter of America
sparrows eat my cherry pits
and throw the fruit-flesh over their shoulders
I'm alone to the right
alone to the left
why didn't I bring my shadow?

——

Draw your fear, the wind said to me
I drew an invasion of silent grass
what do they draw in countries that have no minarets?
asked a pomegranate tree come on foot from Anatolia

——

The people of America sharpen their cypresses like pencils,
write their children to the north
their windows to the south
draw God from right to left like the desert
with an empty belly like the olive tree

< 9 >

soluble dans l'eau comme le saule
son ombre le précédant
parfois l'inverse quand il prend à la terre l'envie de se retourner

———

Voici ta prison m'ont dit les enfants
en traçant un cercle
autour de mon pied

———

Tu as bien vieilli dit la mère à l'enfant
vu d'en haut tu ressembles à une brindille
vu d'en bas à une écharde de cognassier
ton berceau a rejoint la forêt
Nina s'appuie sur la jarre pour empêcher le lait de tourner

———

Le père dit:
des vents contraires ont raturé l'enfant
la mère tricote un bébé de laine long comme l'année
rond comme un pain cuit entre deux pierres
essaie-le dit-elle à Nina pour savoir s'il a la forme de ton étreinte

———

Le linge sur la corde a suivi la tempête
la mère l'a appelé à travers la grille fermée aux lapins
le corsage de soie blanc battait des ailes
le drap de noces flottait au-dessus du cimetière
le cœur de Nina et les volets s'arrachaient à leurs gonds

———

Le vent dit-elle œuvre en cercles fermés avec sa panoplie d'objets
    ronds:
casseroles invisibles
parapluies transis

< 10 >

soluble in water like the willow
with his shadow preceding him
and sometimes the other way round when the earth gives him a
     taste for turning

——

Here is your prison the children said to me
drawing a circle
around my foot

——

How you've aged says the mother to the child
seen from above you look like a vine shoot
seen from below like a pine needle
your cradle went back to the forest
Nina leans on the jug to keep the milk from turning

——

The father says:
contrary winds have crossed out the child
the mother is knitting a woolen baby as long as the year
round as a loaf of bread baked between two stones
try it on she says to Nina to see if it's same the shape as your
     lovemaking

——

The laundry on the line followed the wind
the mother called after it from behind the gate closed to keep out
     rabbits
the white silk blouse flapped its wings
the wedding sheet floated above the cemetery
Nina's heart and the shutters tore away from their hinges

——

The wind she says works in closed circles with its set of round
     objects
invisible saucepans
pierced umbrellas

< 11 >

miroirs de poche
ses cris tassent les haies où s'abritent des vents femelles
pourquoi le vent n'a-t-il pas de maison?

———

Où vas-tu comme ça?
a demandé la porte à la mère
ramener la maison à la maison pour la fin du deuil

———

Les sept lunes de la semaine sont les amies de la maison
c'est pour elles que la mère plonge la cannelle dans le lait bouillant
que Nina rase l'herbe blonde de ses aisselles
pour les honorer que le jardinier tourne autour de son balai

———

La lune, dit-il, est lucarne de Mahomet
c'est le Prophète qui a taillé le cyprès en crayon à papier
lui qui a ordonné au papyrus d'écrire le livre des morts
et donné au chêne la sueur des hommes quand
les femmes relèvent leurs jupes pour contenir le feu des braseros

———

Le père écrit une lettre à la vitesse du vent
Nina dit-il est amoureuse jusqu'aux yeux
c'est visible à sa manière d'enfiler les poivrons comme des baisers
Grand-père n'a pas fermé l'œil de la nuit
il y avait réception au cimetière et porte ouverte à l'étang
il paraît que les âmes égarées et les insectes prolifèrent dans l'eau
   inerte

———

Donnez-moi des ciseaux pour couper les cheveux du camphrier
dit la mère qui n'a ni ciseaux ni camphrier

———

< 12 >

pocket mirrors
its cries thicken the hedges where the female winds take shelter
why doesn't the wind have a house?

——

Where are you going looking like that?
the door asked the mother
to bring the house home for the end of mourning

——

The week's seven moons are friends of the household
it's for them that the mother plunges cinnamon in boiling milk,
that Nina shaves the blonde grass of her armpits,
to honor them that the gardener circles around his broom

——

The moon he says is Mohammed's skylight
it's the Prophet who sharpened the cypress into a pencil to write with
he who ordered the papyrus to write the book of the dead
and gave to the oak men's sweat when
women raise their skirts to hold back the fire of the braziers

——

The father writes a letter as quickly as the wind
Nina, he says, is in love up to her eyes
You can see it in the way she skewers the peppers like kisses
Grandfather didn't close his eyes all night long
there was a cocktail party at the cemetery and open house in the
    pond
it seems that strayed souls and insects proliferate in stagnant water

——

Give me a pair of scissors to cut the camphor tree's hair
says the mother who has neither scissors nor camphor tree

——

< 13 >

Quatre murs avait la maison répète Nina
quatre côtés la boîte d'allumettes
et quatre enfants moins un qui alla rejoindre la portée de chats
    dans le puits

———

Approche-toi de la fenêtre si tu veux confondre l'air accroupi par
    terre
associer le puits à ton deuil
libérer la cigale de la boîte d'allumettes
effacer l'empreinte de l'enfant sur l'eau

———

Odeur humide des sanglots
sèche de la jarre adossée à la porte
sur le seuil étréci au centre
la chatte est lourde de lait inutile
le soir pèse sur sa nuque raidie par l'attente
l'année, se dit-elle, sera retournée

———

Même silence des chatons et du puits
la colère du père renverse la maison
personne ne ramasse les débris de l'encrier
la lampe n'applaudit plus avec les lucioles
nous sommes riches de quatre murs
nous ne partageons la lune avec personne
ni ne consolons aucun nuage
Un nuage c'est fait pour pleurer

———

La lune maigrit à vue d'œil dit la mère
elle est exsangue
j'ai vu les chiens laper son sang sur le talus
le facteur à sa vue arrête sa tournée
il apportera demain la lettre rouge au paillasson

< 14 >

Four walls had the house Nina would repeat
four sides the box of matches
and four children minus one who went to join the litter of kittens
    in the well

———

Come close to the window if you want to fool the air crouched on
    the ground
include the well in your mourning
free the cricket from the matchbox
erase the child's imprint on the water

———

Damp odor of sobs
dry odor of the jug with its back against the door
on the threshold shrunk in the center
the cat is heavy with useless milk
evening weighs on her neck stiffened with waiting
the year, she says to herself, will be turned around

———

The same silence from the kittens and the well
the father's anger overturns the house
no one picks up the shards of the inkwell
the lamp no longer applauds with the fireflies
we are endowed with four walls
we don't share the moon with anyone
or console any cloud
A cloud is made for weeping

———

The moon is shrinking away before our eyes says the mother
it is pale and bloodless
I saw dogs lapping up its blood on the hillside
The postman stops his rounds at the sight of it
tomorrow he will bring the red letter to the doormat

< 15 >

les graines jaunes au merle
demain il échangera sa bicyclette contre un âne tout neuf

———

À quoi attacherons-nous l'ombre maintenant que nous n'avons
    plus ni âne ni cerisier?
demande la mère

< 16 >

yellow grains to the blackbird
tomorrow he'll trade his old bicycle for a brand-new donkey

———

Where will we tie up the cherry tree's shadow
now that we have neither donkey nor cherry tree?
asks the mother

< 17 >

ORTIES

< 18 >

NETTLES

I.

Noircir les pages jusqu'à épuisement des mots et surgissement de
    ce personnage que je vois pour la première fois
Je ne connais pas son nom
inutile de le lui demander
il ne sait pas écrire
il ne sait pas parler non plus
il sait seulement qu'il est né du contact de la plume et du papier
du voisinage de deux mots que le hasard a mis côte à côte
il se laisse faire lorsque je l'installe au milieu de la ligne entre un
    verbe et un objet
mais l'écarte un rien lorsqu'il essaie d'occuper tout le terrain
et fais la sourde oreille lorsqu'il tente de m'entraîner dans l'action
j'ai décidé d'être seule maître du jeu

Suspendue au milieu de la page
j'attends un deuxième personnage pour prendre ma décision
sa parution ne saurait tarder
c'est visible aux remous qui agitent la ligne
au mouvement de vagues qui la traversent de bout en bout
un mot va surgir des profondeurs
mot différent des autres
je crie dans sa direction mais il ne m'entend pas
il se retourne
secoue la tête comme si mes appels étaient formulés dans une
    langue étrangère
me conseille de m'adresser un étage plus bas
à la ligne suivante
puis me glisse subrepticement le mot de passe «ORTIES» pour
    faciliter ma tâche

«Retiens-le sinon tu passeras ta vie dans la marge
les pages c'est pareil aux gares

< 20 >

I.

Blackening pages till words exhaust themselves and this character
    emerges, whom I'm seeing for the first time
I don't know his name
useless to ask him
he doesn't know how to write
he doesn't know how to speak either
he only knows that he's born of the pen's contact with the page
of the proximity of two words which chance has placed side by side
He lets me have my way when I park him in the middle of the line
    between a verb and an object
but I push him away a bit when he tries to take up the whole space
and turn a deaf ear when he tries to goad me into action
I have decided you're the one who makes the rules of the game

Suspended in the middle of the page
I wait for a second character so you can make up your mind
his appearance isn't long coming
it's visible in the ripples that ruffle the line
in the waves' movement crossing it from one end to the either
a word will emerge from the depths
a word different from all the others
I cry out in his direction but he doesn't hear me
he turns around
shakes his head as if I had been calling out in a foreign language
advises me to place your request one floor down
on the next line
then surreptitiously slips you the password NETTLES to make my
    task easier

—Remember it, or you'll pass your whole life in the margin
the pages are like train stations

< 21 >

les rails obéissent à une logistique précise
les déplacer change la perspective
tu perdras ton voyageur

Celui que tu attends de tout temps. Ton personnage principal

Il détient toutes les ficelles car tout converge vers lui
tu le reconnaîtras à l'odeur»

Une vieille femme pliée jusqu'au sol arrache à mains nues
l'ortie qui a poussé sur la page puis la lance dans la marge
elle s'arrête pour me crier qu'elle était ma mère
je suis forcée de la croire à cause de l'ortie
C'était hier
il y a plus d'un demi-siècle
l'hiver venu
les orties montaient à l'assaut de nos fenêtres
interdisaient au jour de pénétrer dans les chambres
narguaient la lampe à pétrole
la femme qui était notre mère partageait avec nous la même odeur
     d'herbe jamais coupée et mêmes pluies
elle remettait toujours au lendemain ce travail qu'elle disait au-
     dessus de ses forces
C'est une fois morte qu'elle retroussa ses manches pour leur faire
     un sort
ses ahanements ne sont pas signe de fatigue mais de satisfaction
     devant le travail accompli
«j'aurais dû le faire de mon vivant», explique-t-elle sur un ton
     d'excuse
en s'essuyant le front avec le coin de son tablier
geste qui montre l'étendue de sa robe rongée par son séjour sous
     terre

< 22 >

the rails obey their own logistics
shifting them changes the perspective
you risk losing your traveler

The one you've always been waiting for. Your main character

the one who holds all the strings, on whom everything converges
the one whose odor you'll recognize

An old woman bent right down to the ground pulls out with her
    bare hands
the nettle which has sprouted on the page then throws it in the
    margin
She stops to shout out to me that she was my mother
I'm obliged to believe her because of the nettle
It was yesterday
that is to say forty years ago
when winter came
the nettles mounted an assault on our windows
forbade the daylight to enter the narrow rooms
taunted the oil lamp
the woman who was our mother shared with us the same smell of
    eternally uncut grass and the same continual rain
she always put off till tomorrow those tasks she said were beyond
    her strength
but now that she's dead she rolls up her sleeves to make short work
    of them
her puffing and panting aren't a sign of fatigue
but of satisfaction at a job well done
"I should have done this when I was alive," she explains in an
    apologetic tone
wiping her face with a corner of her apron
a gesture which reveals how much damage was done to her dress
    by the damp and the earth

< 23 >

Elle parle pour parler
son silence pouvant être mal interprété
faire croire qu'elle est morte
elle parle pour remplir la page
et débarrasser le terrain vague de ses mauvaises herbes
déterrer du même geste les poèmes du fils

Elle dit des choses sans importance
et les années lui tombent dessus à mesure qu'elle parle
une ride par phrase

Les orties sont des vieilles connaissances
des voisines dénuées de grâce hébergées par charité
elle avait pitié d'elles une fois l'an
quand l'automne tournait le dos à l'hiver
sa sympathie allait au grenadier qui saignait sur le mur de la cuisine
ses menstrues lui revenaient par le biais de l'arbre qui la regardait le
    regarder
pourtant elle n'était pas si âgée à l'époque
c'est une fois morte qu'elle a vieilli d'un coup
lorsqu'elle dut traverser le pays en guerre pour se faire enterrer
    dans sa montagne
un village étroit
les hommes remplaçaient les arbres
les femmes étaient l'herbe

Plantée au pied d'un mûrier mâle
elle retourna à la ville décolorée par les pluies
comment fit-elle pour parcourir douze mille kilomètres de haine
«il fallait le faire» dit-elle modeste

mais elle a beau faucher
l'ortie arrachée croît plus vite que ses gestes

< 24 >

She talks just to talk
her silence could be taken wrong
make it seem as if she were dead
she talks to fill up the page
and to weed the empty lot
dig up her son's poems with the same movement

She says insignificant things
and the years drop from her as she speaks
a wrinkle for every sentence

the nettles are old acquaintances
acrimonious neighbors lacking all grace whom she took in out of
    charity
she took pity on them once a year
when autumn turned its back on winter
her sympathy went to the pomegranate tree which bled on the
    kitchen wall
her menstrual flow came back to her through the tree that
    watched her watching it
yet she wasn't all that old at the time
it was once she was dead that she suddenly aged
when it was necessary to cross a country at war to be buried on
    her mountain
a narrow village
the men replaced the trees
the women were the grass

Planted at the foot of a male mulberry tree
She returned to the rain-bleached city
what got into her to cross 1200 kilometers of hate
"I had to do it," she said modestly

But all her weeding was useless
the uprooted nettles grew faster than she could pull them out

< 25 >

Arrivée un mercredi soir
elle ne put compter sur l'aide de personne
campée dans sa fatigue
elle enchaînait le jour à la nuit
consciente qu'elle pouvait remourir
sans avoir enterré nos cris et le linge sanglant du grenadier
les voisins la voyaient ahaner
distraits par le vacarme du vent qui tambourinait sur leurs volets
du soleil qui s'étrécissait de jour en jour
on l'oubliait quand la nuit transformait le ciel en tôle ondulée
on lui donnait des noms de coléoptères
on l'assimilait à l'araignée qui consomme époux après époux

Un passant étranger à la ville la prit pour une personne vivante
        mais pas beaucoup
«elle fera mieux de mourir et de laisser sa place à une ortie»
        suggéra-t-il

Le mot ORTIE me ramène à mon point de départ
je vais devoir aller à la ligne
ou reprendre une autre page
avouer que rien de ce que j'ai décrit n'est vrai
impossible pour une vieille femme de surcroît morte de revenir à
        pied dans une ville honnie pour déterrer larmes et poèmes
et faucher des orties qui la narguaient lorsque les insomnies la
        jetaient vers la fenêtre
d'où elle avait vue sur le mauvais côté de la nuit

< 26 >

She arrived on a Wednesday evening
she couldn't count on anyone's help
encamped in her fatigue
she ran the day on into the night
aware that she could die all over again
without having buried our cries and the pomegranate tree's bloody
    linens
the neighbors saw her puffing and panting
distracted by the noise of the wind drumming on their shutters
by the sun which shrank from day to day
they forgot her when night turned the sky to undulating sheet
    metal
they called her by the names of beetles
likened her to the spider who devours husband after husband

A foreign passerby took her for someone alive, but not very
"she'd do better to die and leave her place to a nettle" he opined

The word NETTLE brings me back to my starting point
I must go right to the end of the line
or begin another page
admit that nothing I've described here is true
that it's impossible for an old woman, a dead one at that, to return
    on foot to a despised city to unearth tears and poems
and pull up the nettles that mocked her when insomnia pulled her
    to the window
from which she had a view of the bad side of the night

< 27 >

II.

Pourtant
il m'arrive de trouver crédible ce voyage de la morte et des mots
d'apprécier ses efforts de jardinage
les orties amassées dans l'angle d'une page
elle interpellait les vivants barricadés derrière la nuit
la mer cachée dans les maisons
clamant haut les noms
avant de regagner son sombre réduit sous le mûrier mâle

Sage décision
il était temps qu'elle cédât sa place à d'autres
aux voisins témoins de l'étroitesse de sa vie et des murs
de l'impossibilité de débarrasser le terrain des jeunes orties plus
        résistantes que les vieilles

Des voix s'élèvent entre les lignes
elles réclament le personnage principal vu sa connaissance
        cadastrale des lieux
je dis connaissance pour ne pas dire terreur
pour ne pas dire enfouissement sous terre quand le père décidait
        d'enterrer le fils et ses poèmes sous les orties

Que sont devenus les passants les sœurs?
Trois sœurs réunies en une seule qui tient la plume
la fait courir sur la page
et la page se met à parler
la page dit:
encrier renversé
lampe brisée
pétrole en flammes
incendie
voisins guettant dans la marge
alignés face à la fenêtre avec leurs seaux
ils conseillent au père de garder sa colère pour le jour

< 28 >

II.

And yet
I can believe in this dead woman's journey with words
appreciate her efforts at gardening
the nettles amassed in the corner of a page
she called out to the living barricaded behind the night
the sea hidden in their houses
shouting out their names
before going back to her dark cupboard beneath the male mulberry
    tree

Wise decision
it was time to give up her place to others
to the neighbors who knew how narrow were her life and her walls
and how impossible to rid her yard of young nettles, hardier than
    the old ones

Voices rise between the lines
they demand the main character, given her land-office knowledge
    of the place
I say knowledge so as not to say terror
so as not to say retreat underground when the father decided to
    bury the son and his poems under the nettles

What became of the passersby, the sisters?
Three sisters united in one who holds the pen
makes it race across the page
and the page begins to speak
the page says:
overturned inkwell
broken lamp
oil ablaze
fire
neighbors peering through the margin
lined up outside the window with their buckets
they advise the father to keep his anger for the daytime

< 29 >

ses cris rayent le ciel
font fuir la lune
qui rebrousse chemin à l'approche de notre toit

Pourtant
la même lune s'est fixée sur le mûrier mâle
plus un seul être dans le village
les vivants sont au cimetière

des maisons au nombre des lettres de l'alphabet
majuscules de pierre sur la pente
lettres de torchis sur le bord du ravin
c'est là qu'œuvrait le frère de la mère
charpentier le jour
constructeur de cercueils la nuit
caisses longitudinales adossées aux murs telles horloges vides
glu mijotant dans chaudron vêtu de suie centenaire

la mort de sa sœur l'a-t-elle affecté?
les lèvres se retournent
les enfants tirent les jupes de leurs mères

la chèvre égorgée sous l'eau de la fontaine évacue son dernier
    soubresaut
le frère devait être dans la foule
mais comme tout le monde se ressemble
le soleil tanne uniformément les visages
la neige cinq mois de l'année creuse les mêmes rides
seul Lucas se détachait de la masse
le vieil instituteur suivait le convoi de la montagne
de la pente qu'il arpentait à pas lents
un rien solennel
un demi-siècle et une guerre en ont fait un rancunier à vie
Lucas aima la morte

< 30 >

his shouting stripes the sky
drives the moon away
which would turn in its tracks when it saw our roof come near

And yet
the same moon stands above the male mulberry tree
not a soul left in the village
the living are all in the cemetery

as many houses as there are letters of the alphabet
capitals in stone on the slope
letters of mortar at the edge of the ravine
it was there that my mother's brother worked
carpenter by day
coffin maker by night
long cartons stacked upright on the wall like empty clocks
glue simmering in a cauldron decked in centenarian soot

did his sister's death affect him?
his lips turn back
children pull on their mothers' skirts

the goat whose throat was slit beneath the fountain shudders one
    last time
the brother must be among the crowd
but everyone looks alike
the sun tans all their faces equally
five months of snow every year creases the same wrinkles
only Lucas stood out in the crowd
the old schoolmaster followed the procession from the mountain
to the slope he paced down in even steps
a bit solemn
half a century and a war have given him a life-long grudge
Lucas loved the dead woman

< 31 >

Quel chemin emprunta-t-il un demi-siècle auparavant pour
    atteindre le village
personne ne l'avait vu arriver
le chemin de la vallée bloqué par neiges et loups
celui de la montagne non encore tracé par le vent

debout au milieu de la place
les pieds joints sur une plaque de gel
il se tenait à un jet de pierres entre la mercerie qui vendait des
    ficelles des cordelettes des pelotes de laine
et l'épicerie où s'entassaient par ordre de poussière
les boîtes de conserve, boîtes d'allumettes, bougies

Étaient-ce les autorités qui l'avaient nommé dans ce village
qui comptait autant de chèvres que d'élèves
autant de cascades que de curés

Une chose était certaine
Lucas venait d'ailleurs
peut-être du même trou de cimetière que son prédécesseur
une cure de jouvence sous terre
le voilà aussi frais qu'un bouton de gardénia
aussi luisant qu'un sou neuf

à leur langage réduit à des mots utilitaires
il opposa le sien riche de plus de cent mots

planté entre la mercerie et l'épicerie
il semblait un prolongement du soleil pendu au-dessus de sa tête
    comme ampoule électrique

Quelle entente possible entre l'homme qui parlait bas et la foule
    parlant plus haut que la cascade
aux balbutiements de ses lèvres
ils comprirent qu'il allait enseigner trois alphabets à leurs enfants

< 32 >

What road had he taken fifty years earlier to reach
    the village
no one had seen him arrive
the road from the valley was blocked by snow and wolves
the one down the mountain not yet marked out by the wind

standing in the middle of the village square
his feet together on a block of ice
he was a stone's throw from the notions shop which sold thread
    and string and skeins of wool
and the grocery where, by rank of their dustiness, were stacked
canned goods, boxes of matches, candles

What officials had sent him to this village
which had as many goats as schoolchildren
as many waterfalls as priests?

One thing was certain
Lucas came from elsewhere
perhaps from the same hole in the cemetery as his predecessor
a sojourn in the underground spa
and there he was as fresh as a gardenia bud
shiny as a new penny

to their language, shrunken to useful words
he contrasted his, rich with more than a hundred

planted between the notions shop and the grocery
he seemed like an extension of the sun hanging above his head like
    a light bulb

What understanding was possible between the man who spoke
    softly and the crowd talking louder than the waterfalls
from his stammering
they understood that he would teach their children three alphabets

< 33 >

Le grec parce que tout vient de là
l'araméen à cause du Christ
le français pour venger Jeanne d'Arc et Vercingétorix

Superflue la langue du pays
la guerre l'effacera
il tombera dans le ravin
se liquéfiera dans le fleuve
un trou le remplacera sur les cartes géographiques

Mais d'où venait-il pour parler avec autant d'autorité?
sa main frappa l'air au-dessus de son épaule
il venait de derrière son propre dos
du nord
n'importe quel nord
d'Antioche du lac de Van du détroit de Béring
pourvu qu'il vînt de quelque part

«C'est comment la ville»
lui demanda-t-on
«la mer mange-t-elle encore la terre»
impatient de dispenser le savoir et de planter son drapeau sur la
     fronton de l'école
Lucas fit celui qui n'avait pas entendu

Il enseignait d'une voix tonitruante
aussi haute que les murs du cimetière
imprégnait les mots de sa salive pour les enrober de leur jus
trois alphabets alors qu'il neigeait cinq mois l'an
alphabets balayés comme crottes de chèvre lorsque la mère partit

Lucas empila les bancs sur les pupitres
décrocha le drapeau
inscrivit sur le tableau noir trois mots:
«je suis mort»

< 34 >

Greek because everything came from there
Aramaic because of the Christ
and French to avenge Joan of Arc and Vercingétorix

The language of their country was superfluous
war would erase it
it would tumble into the ravine
be liquefied in the river
a hole would replace it on maps of the world

But where did he come from to speak with such authority?
his hand struck the air above his shoulder
he came from behind his own back
from the north
no matter what north
from Antioch to the lake of Van to the Bering Strait
as long as he came from somewhere

"What's it like in the city?"
they asked him
"Does the sea still eat up the land?"
impatient to dispense knowledge and to put up his flag on the
    schoolhouse pediment
Lucas pretended not to have heard

He taught with a booming voice
as high as the cemetery walls
steeped words in his saliva to coat them in their own juice
three alphabets while it snowed five months out of the year
alphabets swept away like goat turds when the mother left

Lucas piled the benches up on the school desks
took down the flag
wrote three words on the blackboard:
"I am dead"

< 35 >

L'annonce de la mort de la mère me jette dans la rue
je m'adresse aux passants dans son dialecte âpre comme fruit de
    jujubier
crie pour écarter l'air qui entrave ma marche
me tais pour m'entendre pleurer
ramasse les larmes devenues pierreuses et les branches cassées
j'en ferai un feu alors que je n'ai ni cheminée ni mots à brûler

À genoux devant l'âtre
la mère injuriait les flammes quand un sarment trop vert faisait des
    étincelles
elle avait un compte à régler avec le froid
avec ses reins
quatre enfants suspendus à ses hanches
un sol vomisseur de boue et de poussière
le balai fidèle compagnon
quitté à ras de tombe

Armée d'une plume et d'un plumeau j'essaie de la tirer vers la
    maison des orties
Mais elle lâche ma main

Elle fait cause commune avec un mûrier et un merle œuvrant
    entre écorce et aubier
«ménage-toi lui répète-t-elle
ton chant est plus long que ton souffle
laisse l'ortie enterrer les orties»

sa maison a suivi une fleur en pot
il y a la porte mais pas les murs
le vent mais pas les fenêtres
sa maison est morte comme tout ce qui marche:
l'homme le ruisseau le chemin
le sol s'est approprié les odeurs
celle noire de l'encre renversée

< 36 >

The announcement of the mother's death drove me out into the
    street
I talk to passersby in her dialect sour as jujube fruit
cry out to push aside the air that binds my stride
grow silent to hear myself weep
gather up my stony tears with the broken branches
I'll make a fire with them, though I've neither fireplace nor words
    to burn

Kneeling before the hearth
the mother swore at the flames when a too-green shoot made
    sparks
she had a score to settle with the cold
with her loins
four children hanging to her hips
a floor that vomited mud and dust
the broom her faithful companion
left at the graveside

Armed with a pen and a feather-duster I try to drag her toward the
    house of the nettles
But she drops my hand

She joins forces with a mulberry tree and a blackbird working
    between bark and sapwood
"take it easy," she tells him
"your song is longer than your breath
let the nettle bury the nettles"

her house followed a potted flower
there was a door but no walls
a wind but no windows
her house was dead like everything that walks:
a man a stream a road
the floor had grabbed up all the odors
the black one of spilled ink

< 37 >

rouge des herbes séchées sur la rambarde
jaune du persil qui active le sang récalcitrant
épaisse de la menthe contre les nausées
sinueuse du safran qui fait pâlir le riz
et de la verveine capable d'apaiser la colère

< 38 >

the red one of herbs dried on the railing
yellow of parsley that livens sluggish blood
thick odor of mint against nausea
sinuous saffron that bleaches rice
and verbena that calms anger

< 39 >

III.

C'était hier
il y a très longtemps
la colère du père renversait la maison
nous nous cachions derrière les dunes pour émietter ses cris
la Méditerranée tournait autour de nous comme chien autour d'un
    mendiant
la mère nous appelait jusqu'au couchant

ça devait être beau et ce n'était que triste
les jardins trépassaient plus lentement que les hommes
nous mangions notre chagrin jusqu'à la dernière miette
puis le rotions échardes à la face du soleil

C'était ailleurs
il y a très longtemps
lasse de nous appeler
la mère quitta la terre pour entrer dans la terre
vue d'en haut elle ressemblait à un caillou
vue d'en bas à une pomme de pin écaillée
il lui arrivait de pleurer en sanglots qui faisaient frémir le feuillage
la vie lui criions-nous est une ligne droite de bruits
la mort un cercle vide
dehors il y a l'hiver
la mort d'un moineau a noirci la neige
mais rien ne la consolait

Quelle est la nuit parmi les nuits demandait-elle à la chouette
mais la chouette ne pense pas
la chouette sait

nous pensions à elle tous les jours
puis une fois la semaine
puis une fois l'an
dans une photo ses cheveux sont couleur sépia
les morts vieillissent comme le papier

< 40 >

III.

It was yesterday
it was long ago
the father's anger overturned the house
we would hide behind the dunes to shred his shouting
the Mediterranean prowled around us like a dog circling a beggar
the mother called us until sunset

it should have been beautiful and it was merely sad
gardens departed this life more slowly than men
we would eat our sorrow down to the last drop then
belch it in splinters in the face of the cold

It was elsewhere
it was a very long time ago
tired of calling us
the mother left the earth to enter the earth
seen from above she looked like a pebble
seen from below she looked like a flaking pinecone
sometimes she wept in sobs that made the foliage tremble
life, we cried out to her, is a straight line of noises
death an empty circle
outside there is winter
the death of a sparrow has blackened the snow
but nothing consoled her

What is the night among all nights? she asked the owl
but the owl doesn't think
the owl knows

we would think about her every day
then once a week
then once a year
in a photo her hair was sepia
the dead age like paper

< 41 >

Ça ne pouvait être qu'ailleurs
la colère du soleil renversait le pays
des hommes venus du côté sourd du fleuve cognaient aux
    frontières
je dis hommes pour ne pas dire sauterelles
je dis sauterelles pour ne pas dire fétus de paille fanes de maïs

leur sueur avait l'acidité de l'armoise
leur haleine l'amertume du cyprès

Ils arrivèrent tous les soirs de toutes les années
leurs arbres en laisse
leurs enfants plantés au pied de leurs oliviers
dans son sombre réduit la mère comptait leurs pas
la mère compatissait
leurs langues épaissies par le sel de la mer Morte
leurs gorges emplies du vent de la Galilée
ils creusèrent leurs tranchées dans nos chambres
allongèrent leurs fusils entre nos draps
squattèrent nos trottoirs à longueur d'homme
à longueur de honte
leur torpeur une fois morts ne les a pas suivis

Visible à travers le linge sur nos cordes leur pays leur tourne le dos

< 42 >

It could only have been elsewhere
the sun's anger overturned the country
men who came from the wounded side of the river knocked on
    our borders
I say men so as not to say locusts
I say locusts so as not to say wisps of straw, corn silk

their hands had the acidity of tarragon
their breath the bitterness of cypress trees

They arrived every night of every year
their trees on leashes
their children planted at the foot of their olive trees
in her dark cupboard the mother counted their steps
counted the wing-casings of their rustling bodies
the mother sympathized
their tongues thickened by the salt of the Dead Sea
their throats filled with the wind of Galilee
they dug their trenches in our bedrooms
stretched their rifles out in our beds
squatted our sidewalks for the length of a man's life
for the length of shame
their torpor, once they were dead, did not follow them

Visible through the washing on our clotheslines, their country
    turns its back on them

< 43 >

Cachez la maison derrière la maison
enterrez la terre dans la terre
les étrangers emporteront les murs comme fagots de bois au dos
    de leurs mulets
boiront la sueur verte des arbres
l'urine noire des mines
le sang gris des rochers
le pays sous leurs pieds glissera vers le nord
le sud bardé de barbelés deviendra ouest

des voleuses leurs femmes cousant leur luzerne sur nos prés
un mensonge leurs brebis fécondées sept fois l'an
et que leurs oreillers s'envolent avec les cigognes
trop courtes leurs échelles pour quérir la pluie
leur chanvre effiloché
ils naissent et meurent à la lueur des lanternes

Adossés à l'air froid
ils voient des choses s'approcher
je dis choses pour ne pas dire silhouettes
ce ne sont pas des silhouettes non plus
mais les contours improbables d'êtres promenant leur désarroi

Un soir
dans l'embrasure de notre porte apparut un homme aux cils blancs
l'eau du robinet gela après son depart

< 44 >

Hide the house behind the house
bury the earth in the earth
the strangers will carry the walls away like firewood on their
    mules' backs
they will drink the trees' green sweat
the mines' black urine
the rocks' gray blood
the country beneath their feet will slide north
bound in barbed wire the south will become the west

thieves, their women sewing their alfalfa into our fields
lies, their ewes bearing seven times in a year
let their pillows fly off with the storks
their ladders are too short to fetch the rain
their hemp is frayed
they are born and die by lantern light

Their backs against the cold air
they see things approaching
I say things so as not to say shadows
but they are not shadows either
they are the unlikely shapes of beings walking their confusion

one night
a man with white eyelashes appeared in our doorway
the water in the faucets froze when he left

< 45 >

IV.

À quelle ligne et quelle page commence leur migration
s'interroge la mère
faut-il la relier aux fenêtres qui se mirent à se dévisager
aux pluies qui sautèrent sur notre toit à pieds joints
la mère n'avait ni crayon ni ardoise pour compter leurs sauts
la mère ne savait pas compter
elle les prit pour des chats alors qu'ils étaient des guerriers
ils n'étaient pas des guerriers non plus mais des lignes courbes
    marchant dans leur sommeil

Propos de peu d'importance
courant comme feu follet sur une herbe sèche
tenus par celle qui soliloque sous terre
sa voix imite les pierres par temps d'avalanche et de pénurie d'air

Les jardiniers qui redoutent les incendies
creusent un trou
le remplissent à ras bord d'abeilles
reviennent le lendemain
jettent le miel aux fourmis
serrent le bourdonnement dans un balluchon

ils marchent les pieds écartés de peur d'être repérés par le feu
et la solitude enveloppe la morte qui réclame un miroir pour se
    recoiffer
de peur que le bourdon ne la prenne pour une mendiante

Demain il fera jour
dit-elle chaque fois qu'un soleil avale un soleil
demain les visiteurs s'en iront à leur tour avec les chemins
comme les murs
comme les enfants
Dieu sait où

< 46 >

IV.

At what line and on what page did their migration begin
the mother asks herself
ought one to connect it to the windows which reflect and stare at
    each other
to the rains which jump feet together on our roof
the mother had neither pencil nor blackboard to count their leaps
the mother didn't know how to count
she took them for cats when they were warriors
they weren't warriors either but curved lines walking in their sleep

Statements of small importance
spreading like phosphorous fire on dry grass
made by someone who soliloquizes underground
her voice imitates the stones in seasons of avalanches and lack of air

The gardeners who fear fires
dig a hole
fill it to the brim with bees
come back the next day
throw the honey to the ants
tie the buzzing up in a bundle

they walk with their feet wide apart for fear of being spotted by the
    fire
and solitude wraps the dead woman who asks for a mirror to redo
    her hair
for fear that the drone will mistake her for a beggar

Tomorrow it will be day
she says each time a sun devours a sun
tomorrow the visitors will go away in turn taking their roads with
    them
like the walls
like the children
God knows where

< 47 >

Appuyée sur le manche de son balai tel le Giaour ottoman sur sa
    baïonnette
la mère échangerait sa vie contre un livre
La nuit dit-elle est un tableau noir
donnez-moi un crayon pour vous écrire une lettre
quel temps faisait-il le jour de mon enterrement?
Avait-on prévu des chaises pour les visiteurs suivis de chiens
avait-on moulu du café pour les insomniaques?
s'essuyaient-ils les pieds sur le paillasson avant de traverser le seuil?
Le marc de café lui tenait lieu de seule lecture
elle disait nuit
et nous ramassions linge et nuages suspendus à la corde

elle disait mer
et nous nous hissions jusqu'à la lucarne et
cette odeur laiteuse de vagues jamais vues de près

elle disait cavité brèche et
nous creusions avec rage pour nous assurer qu'il y avait de la terre
    dans la terre
et qu'il y avait plus humble que nous

elle disait lettre
et nous attendions sur le pas de la porte la mauvaise nouvelle
décès de parent ou de chèvre dans les maisons plombées par la neige

La mère qui allumait la lampe à pétrole tournait le dos au soleil qui
    plongeait deux fois dans le bassin de l'orphelinat
la première fois pour se laver
la deuxième pour soulever son poids de mécontentement

Morte elle continue à lire le marc de café dans ma tasse du matin
Morte
la maison continue à tourner dans sa tête
morte
elle aligne des silences qui n'ont aucun lien entre eux

< 48 >

Leaning on her broomstick like the Turkish Giaour on his bayonet
the mother would exchange her life for a book
Night, she says, is a blackboard
give me a piece of chalk to write you a letter
what was the weather like the day of my burial?
Did they remember to have chairs for visitors who came with dogs?
did they grind coffee for the insomniacs?
did they wipe their feet on the doormat before crossing the
    threshold?
Coffee grounds were her only reading matter
she said night
and we would bring in the laundry and clouds hung out on the line

she said sea
and we would pull ourselves up to the skylight and
that milky odor of waves never seen close up

she said breached cavity and
we would dig furiously to make sure there was earth in the earth
and that there was someone humbler than ourselves

she said letter
and we'd wait on the doorstep for the bad news
the death of a relative or a goat in the snowbound houses

The mother who lit the oil lamp would turn her back to the sun
    which dived twice into the pond at the orphanage
the first time to wash
the second to lift its weight of discontent

Dead, she continues to read the grounds in my morning cup of
    coffee
Dead
the house continues to turn in her head
dead
she lines up unconnected silences

< 49 >

Penchée au-dessus de mon épaule
la morte analphabète surveille ce que j'écris
chaque ligne ajoute une ride sur mon visage
chaque phrase la rapproche d'un pas de la maison des ORTIES
Elle l'aurait atteinte si les oiseaux n'avaient picoré les cailloux sur
    son parcours
elle dit oiseaux pour ne pas dire guerre
elle dit guerre pour ne pas dire folie du fils et du grenadier

Renvoyé de l'asile bombardé
il s'accroupit au pied de l'arbre qui saignait avec sa mère
personne ne le reconnut
personne ne le chassa
c'était la guerre et la maison avait perdu sa porte
«Ma'man» dit-il en deux temps
il réclamait à la morte les poèmes écrits avant l'asile
alors qu'elle lui avait interdit de prononcer ce mot
ses filles lui resteraient sur les bras
personne ne les épouserait

quelle idée de réclamer des poèmes écrits avant les bombardements
«Tu en écriras d'autres moins démodés
sans gribouillage sans ratures
à la troisième personne pour qu'on ne te reconnaisse pas
au présent pour faire table rase du passé»
voilà ce qu'elle aurait pu dire

Deux morts acrimonieux discutent dans ma tête
«qui parle là-haut?»
une pluie drue répond à ma question
évoquer des morts insatisfaits suffit pour apporter le mauvais
    temps

Nos cris me suivent en haletant
changer de pays et de ville ne sert à rien

< 50 >

Bent over my shoulder
the illiterate dead woman watches over what I write
each line adds a wrinkle to my face
each sentence brings her one step closer to the house of NETTLES
She would have reached it if the birds hadn't pecked up the pebbles
    on her path
she says birds so as not to say war
she says war so as not to say madness of the son and the
    pomegranate tree

Sent home from the bombed asylum
he squatted at the foot of the tree which bled when his mother did
no one recognized him
no one drove him away
there was a war and the house had lost its door
"Ma–ma" he said in two syllables
he wanted the dead woman to give back the poems he wrote
    before the asylum
though she had forbidden him to utter that word
her daughters would stay on her hands forever
no one would marry them

what an idea to ask for poems written before the bombings
"You'll write other ones, more up-to-date
with no scribblings and no crossings-out
in the third person so no one will know it's you
in the present tense to wipe the slate of the past"
that's what she might have said

Two acrimonious dead people argue in my head
"who's talking up there?"
heavy rain answers my question
calling up the discontented dead is enough to bring bad weather

Our cries follow me panting
changing cities or countries does no good

< 51 >

alignés derrière mes fenêtres les voisins morts continuent à
    éteindre l'incendie
alors que le vrai feu était dans nos bouches
dans les reins du père ficelant son fils pour l'enterrer sous les orties
pas de myrrhe ni de benjoin pour le poète qui brandissait ses mots
    telle lanterne dans la tempête
Les seaux d'eau remplaçaient les larmes

Mère de rien du tout
qui traverse les années avec son tablier décoloré
une serpillière dans une main
sa dignité dans l'autre
mère célébrant la nuit avec sa lampe à trois mèches
aplatissant la grisaille
la couchant sur le sol mauvais
en terre battue
pour mieux écouter la respiration des morts
les disputes des vents souterrains

Le temps là-haut était à la contemplation
le linge pouvait attendre
les femmes le suspendaient le lendemain aux cordes
très haut
de peur que les coléoptères n'y fassent leur nid

Immobile face à la ville
la mère bougeait dans ses seuls rêves
enjambait des ruisseaux
piétinait des ronces
houspillait des chacals
lançait des pierres sur les serpents
l'herbe du diable séchait sur les toits avec le thym et le basilic
guérissait les migraines
réconciliait les vents qui s'étripaient dans la vallée
«Jetez-les dehors» criait la mère

< 52 >

lined up outside my windows dead neighbors keep on putting out
   the fire
while the real fire was in our mouths
in the loins of the father tying up his son to bury him under the
   nettles
neither myrrh nor benjamin for the poet who brandished his
   words like a lamp in the storm
Buckets of water took the place of tears

Mother of nothing at all
who crosses the years in her faded apron
a washrag in one hand
her dignity in the other
mother honoring the night with her triple-wicked lamp
beating down the gray weather
laying it down on the bare
earthen floor
the better to hear the breathing of the dead
the arguments of underground winds

Time up above was for contemplation
the laundry could wait
the women would hang it out the next day on very high
   clotheslines
for fear that beetles would nest there

Motionless with the city before her
the mother only traveled in her dreams
stepped across streams
trod on thorns
told off the jackals
threw stones at snakes
the devil's grass dried on the roof with thyme, and basil cured
   migraines
made peace among the winds at each other's throats in the valley
"Throw them out!" the mother would exclaim

< 53 >

il n'y a pas de vent fiable
et elle pédalait de nouveau sur sa machine à coudre
tabliers linceuls robe de mariée se suivaient dans le désordre
elle coupera le fil à la tombée de la nuit
à la tombée de ses paupières cousues d'un fil de feu

Le râteau dans une main
le crayon dans l'autre
je dessine un parterre
écris une fleur à un pétale
désherbe un poème écrit entre veille et sommeil
je fais la guerre aux limaces et aux adjectifs adipeux

le chiendent acrimonieux pousse sur mes draps
les mots récalcitrants se prolongent jusqu'à mon jardin
je sarcle
élague
arrache
replante dans mes rêves
le matin me trouve aussi épuisée qu'un champ labouré par une
    herse rouillée
le rêve seul moyen de locomotion pour atteindre ma mère qui
    habite le dessous

Elle se disait la mère de tous ceux qui savent dessiner une maison
c'est pour eux qu'elle trayait la lune
qu'elle conservait son lait dans une jarre femelle
loin du soleil qui avait mangé ses deux fenêtres
et roté une écharde sur son seuil

Assis sur le même seuil
les mots de ma langue maternelle me saluent de la main
je les déplace avec lenteur comme elle le faisait de ses ustensiles de
    cuisine
marmite écuelle louche bassine ont voyagé de mains en mains

< 54 >

no wind is trustworthy
and she pedaled harder on her sewing machine
aprons shrouds bridal gowns one after another in disorder
she cut the thread when night fell
when her lids dropped sewed shut with a fiery thread

A rake in one hand
a pencil in the other
I draw a flowerbed
write a flower with one petal
weed a poem written between waking and sleeping
I make war on snails and adipose adjectives

bitter couch grass grows between my sheets
recalcitrant words go on down to the garden
I hoe
I prune
I weed
replant in my dreams
morning finds me as exhausted as a field ploughed with a rusty
    harrow
dreams the only means of transportation to reach my mother who
    lives beneath

She said she was the mother of anyone who could draw a house
that she milked the moon for them
kept its milk in a female jug
far from the sun which had eaten her two windows
and belched up a shard on her doorstep

Seated on the same doorstep
the words of my mother tongue wave to me
I move them away slowly the way she did her kitchen utensils
pot soup bowl ladle basin have traveled from hand to hand

< 55 >

quels mots évoquent les migrations d'hommes et de femmes
    fuyant
génocides sécheresse faim
enfants et volailles serrés dans le même balluchon parlaient-ils
l'araméen caillouteux
l'arabe houleux des tribus belliqueuses
ou la langue tintant telles billes de verre dans nos poches d'enfants

< 56 >

what words will recall the migrations of men and women fleeing
genocide drought famine
children and chickens tied up in the same bundle whether they
    spoke
gravelly Aramaic
the choppy Arabic of warring tribes
or the language jingling like marbles in our childhood pockets

< 57 >

INHUMATIONS

< 58 >

INTERMENTS

< 59 >

à Pierre Tabard et Catherine Sellers

À celui qui a enjambé trois montagnes
on donne l'eau des ablutions et une maison assise sur le fleuve
on lui interdit d'adresser la parole à la caillasse
son parler est abrupt ses gesticulations viennent d'un lointain
    alphabet

une jarre vide à portée de sa main
on l'oublie toute une saison entre la pluie qui efface la pluie
et l'écho qui efface l'écho
il était dit qu'il devait repartir
la pointe de ses chaussures était tournée vers la porte

< 60 >

To the man who strode across three mountains
they give water for ablutions and a house seated on the river
they forbid him to say a word to the gravel
his speech is abrupt his movements come from a far-off alphabet

an empty jug is within reach of his hand
for a whole season he is forgotten between the rain which blots out
    the rain
and the echo which drowns out the echo
it was said that he must leave again
the toes of his shoes were facing the door

< 61 >

Ils disent le cercueil étroit
la maison inclinée
personne n'a balayé devant la porte
les neiges chagrinées ont tourné au gel
le lait aussi dans le broc mécontent

Quelqu'un a nourri les hommes du bourg voisin que personne ne
    connaît
descendu l'enfant agrippé à l'échelle
gardé dans un mouchoir la dent de lait

Ce n'est pas par un jour pareil qu'on range la grange
la paille peut attendre
pas la terre entrouverte

< 62 >

They said that the coffin was narrow
the house bent over
no one had swept in front of the doorway
worried snow had turned to ice
the milk in the pitcher was disgruntled

Someone had fed the people in the next town which no one
    had visited
brought down the child who clutched the ladder
kept the baby tooth in a handkerchief

It's not on a day like this that one tidies up the barn
the straw can wait
not the dug-up earth

< 63 >

Couleur miel du cercueil sous le noyer
les clous s'y enfoncent comme dans la soie
l'air est fraternel pour le merle
non pour l'enfant et le soleil assis à l'intersection des branches
vue de cette hauteur
la morte a un air bienveillant
ses mains étaient fébriles hier quand dans un soubresaut de
    rangements
elle ramassa les billes
plia le linge mouillé
sortit le marteau de la boîte à outils
le posa sur la rainure médiane de la table
puis ordonna à l'enfant d'aller promener la nuit en pleine nuit

< 64 >

Honey-color of the coffin under the walnut tree
the nails go into it like silk
the air is fraternal for the blackbird
not for the child and the sun seated in the branches' crotch
seen from that height
the dead woman has a benevolent air
her hands were restless yesterday when in a convulsion of tidying
she gathered the marbles
folded the wet laundry
took a hammer out of the toolbox
placed it on the groove in the middle of the table
then told the child to take the night for a walk at midnight

< 65 >

Le caillou dans la main exprime le chagrin
elle le jette par-dessus son épaule
en prend un autre
léger comme l'âme du défunt
lisse tel genou de fillette sur une balançoire

demain
la terre s'ouvrira pour le besoin d'une inhumation
le vide comblé par des cailloux pris au champ voisin
le deuil partagé aura l'allure d'une fête

< 66 >

A pebble in her hand expresses her grief
she throws it over her shoulder
picks up another
light as the dead man's soul
smooth as the knees of a little girl on a swing

tomorrow
earth will open up for a burial
its emptiness filled by pebbles from a neighboring field
shared mourning will be like a holiday

< 67 >

Femme encerclée par les terres devient épine sous la peau de ceux
    qui s'arrêtaient devant sa haie
ils retournent leur champ et leur cœur
fouillent les sillons
l'appellent rose fiévreuse
œillet d'automne
bruyère taciturne
novembre décape les bras et les outils
jaunit l'air
bleuit la peau des volets
attablés devant un plat de viande crue
les hommes parlent de revenants
alors que l'enfant est éclat de rire derrière la porte

< 68 >

The woman in the midst of her land becomes a thorn beneath the
    skin of those who stop in front of her hedges
they turn over their fields and their hearts
search the furrows
call her fever rose
autumn carnation
stubborn heather
November scrapes clean their arms and tools
yellows the air
blues the skin of the shutters
seated in front of platters of raw meat
men talk of ghosts
while the child is a burst of laughter behind the door

< 69 >

à Andrei Makine

Ils ont salé la neige salé l'agneau du banquet noir
posé une coupe sur le toit pour l'obole de la lune
enfermé l'eau et l'enfant qui éclaboussaient les murs de leurs cris

Ils l'ont serrée dans un drap rêche comme les salines des mers
    pauvres
l'ont emportée sur leurs épaules avec les relents du café et de la
    cardamome prisée par les anges
ils l'ont réunie

Ils ont traversé un désert deux steppes trois dunes et une vallée si
    étroite qu'ils faillirent la renverser
puis enterrée à reculons là où s'arrête le pouls de la terre
à un jet de sanglots de sa cuisine
sous le caroubier inconsolable
avec la bassine rouge des ablutions
les miaulements blancs du chat

Ils la firent voler aussi haut qu'un troupeau de chèvres
de Mésopotamie
plus haut que les cerfs-volants
ils l'ont oubliée

< 70 >

They salted the snow salted the lamb for the black banquet
placed a goblet on the roof for the moon's obol
locked up the water and the child who splashed the walls with
    their cries

They wrapped her in a sheet as rough as the salt marshes of poor
    seas
carried her on their shoulders with dregs of coffee and the
    cardamom favored by angels
they gathered her

They crossed a desert two steppes three dunes and a valley so
    narrow they almost overturned her
then buried her backwards there where the earth's pulse stops
a sob's throw away from her kitchen
under the inconsolable carob tree
with the red washing basin
and the cat's white meowing

They made her fly as high as a flock of goats from Mesopotamia
higher than kites
they forgot her

< 71 >

à Marilyn Hacker

Celle devenue monceau de choses inutiles connaît le chemin
connaît le percheron endimanché lié au bruit des roues
ce n'est pas par un jour pareil qu'on éventre la terre et
ce ne sont pas les oiseaux qui sépareront le blé de l'ivraie
les hommes l'ont saluée puis fauché
ont soulevé leur chapeau puis fauché
Septembre n'admet pas les apitoiements
l'échelle s'impatiente sur le mur de la grange
la pluie prévue avant la mise en terre mouillera le blé
rouillera la herse dans le dernier sillon
les bras sont nécessaires pour hisser les sacs sur le dos de l'air
les fourches en deuil refusent de travailler

< 72 >

For Marilyn Hacker

She who became a pile of useless things knows the way
knows the draft horse in his Sunday best, bound to the wheels'
   racket
it's not on a day like this that they'll disembowel the earth
nor can you leave it to birds to separate the wheat from the chaff
men greeted her then reaped
lifted their hats then reaped
September has no time for pity
the ladder grows impatient on the barn wall
rain predicted before the burial will dampen the wheat
and rust the harrow in the last furrow
arms are needed to hoist the sacks onto the air's back
pitchforks in mourning refuse to work

< 73 >

pour Pierre Brunel

Manches retroussées
vestes accrochées au noyer
ils se mirent à plusieurs pour éventrer la terre
poser la caisse dans le rectangle rouge
avec midi soleil et sueur

ils l'éventrèrent de nouveau à la lumière des torches
sans deuil sans nécessité
l'ombre des pioches sur l'herbe froide dessinait un sextant
le feu brûlait la nuit
la nuit balayait le feu

ils l'auraient éventrée à l'aube sans nord et sans repères
si le sommeil n'avait eu raison des bras et des pioches

< 74 >

For Pierre Brunel

Sleeves rolled up
jackets hung from the walnut tree
several of them got down to work at tearing open the earth
placing the box in the red rectangle
with noon, sun and sweat

they tore it open again by torchlight
neither in mourning nor need
their pickaxes' shadows drew a sextant on the cold grass
fire burned the night
night swept away the fire

they would have torn it open at dawn with no north-point or
    landmark
if sleep had not gotten the better of arms and pickaxes

< 75 >

Les miettes de pain sous la table sont semis de colère jetés par le
    vieillard
il a renversé le jour
renversé l'âtre
fermé l'œil sur le chat qui lapait le feu

Le ciel dit-il est un tapis brûlé par des mégots
la terre est morte mais elle ne le sait pas encore
la terre est en sursis

< 76 >

The breadcrumbs under the table are seeds of anger the old man
        scattered
he has overturned the day
overturned the hearth
closed his eyes to the cat lapping up the fire

The sky he says is a carpet burned by cigarette butts
the earth is dead but doesn't know it yet
the earth is living on borrowed time

< 77 >

Être berger nécessite une parenté de sang avec un loup
des liens avec un brin d'orge ou de luzerne
on échange un fromage contre un bâton
un ballot de laine contre un calendrier
une brebis pleine contre une fille vierge
on apprend l'ignorance aux plantes savantes
l'addition au chien
et au feu de ne pas ronfler en présence des visiteurs

< 78 >

To be a shepherd you must be blood-kin to a wolf
have bonds with a sprig of barley or alfalfa
you exchange a cheese for a staff
a bundle of wool for a calendar
a pregnant ewe for a virgin girl
you teach ignorance to learned plants
teach the dog to add
and the fire not to snore when there are visitors

< 79 >

«Botaniste cherchant perce-neige avec sa loupe n'est pas crédible»
ce qu'il prend pour du brouillard n'est que nuage en herbe
nuage déchu
pour renard n'est que flamme à l'intersection de deux banquises
l'hiver a plus de cent ans
les pays et les livres effacés ont des peines communes
ils se veulent terre d'accueil pour mots gelés
pour oiseaux pétrifiés
alors qu'ils sont linceul et sépulture

< 80 >

"A botanist looking for snowdrops with a magnifying glass isn't
    credible"
what he takes for fog is only a cloud in bud
to a fox
a deposed cloud is only a flame at the intersection of two ice floes
the winter is more than a hundred years old
erased countries and books have the same sorrow
they would like to offer asylum to frozen words
and petrified birds
though they themselves are shroud and sepulcher

< 81 >

Il a un fusil mais pas de crayon
une chamelle aux longs cils mais pas de femme
ses murs les jours impairs s'étrécissent telle boîte d'allumettes

Il part à la guerre lorsqu'un merle arabe attaque son figuier
tourne trois fois autour de son champ
jure que pas un seul mot ne sortira vivant de sa maison

< 82 >

He has a rifle but no pencil
a long-lashed she-camel but no woman
on odd-numbered days his walls shrink down to a matchbox

He goes to war when an Arab blackbird attacks his fig tree
makes the rounds of his field three times
swears that no word will leave his house alive

< 83 >

Elle craint de perdre de vue son image
de ne plus savoir à quoi elle ressemble
de perdre de vue sa maison
de ne plus savoir si la porte s'ouvrait à l'ouest
d'apprendre qu'un chemin a pénétré chez elle
empilé les chaises sur la table
que le platane du rond-point s'accoude sur sa rambarde

sa crainte de ne plus savoir éteindre le soleil
pour évacuer le sanglot à l'étroit dans sa gorge

< 84 >

She is afraid to lose sight of her reflection
to no longer know what she looks like
to lose sight of her house
to no longer know if the door opens to the west
to learn that a road has gotten indoors
piled the chairs up on the table
that the plane tree from the intersection is leaning on her railing

her fear of no longer knowing how to put out the sun
to evict the sob crowded into her throat

< 85 >

L'eucalyptus a les jambes arquées de ceux qui font cause commune
 avec un cheval
ses bûches font grimacer la cheminée
sa sueur acide fait tourner le lait dans les jarres

les abeilles qui promènent leur miel dans l'air ont de bonnes
 raisons pour ne pas s'y poser
ses branches servent de lieu de villégiature aux morts quand le
 soleil brouille noms et dates
la femme qui a une fleur en pot dit
seul meurt ce qui marche
l'homme le ruisseau la fumée

< 86 >

The eucalyptus is bowlegged like those who make common cause
    with horses
its logs make the fireplace creak
its acid sweat makes milk turn in the jug

the bees who parade their honey in the air have good reasons not
    to light on it
its branches serve as a summer home for the dead when the sun
    confuses names and dates
the woman who has a flower in a pot says
only things that walk die
man   brook   smoke

< 87 >

Le deuil durcit les cœurs des fillettes et les mines des crayons
la réserve de kérosène épuisée
les loups mangent celles aux jambes d'allumettes

à qui appartient ce corps nu dans ma nudité demande la terre
qui a posé une braise à l'intersection de la neige et de mes genoux
pourquoi le coq de bruyère appelle-t-il crêtes ses pétales

et pourquoi le mendiant de la place ouvre-t-il sa braguette pour
    recevoir l'aumône de quelques sous

< 88 >

Mourning hardens little girls' hearts and the lead in pencils
when the stock of kerosene is used up
wolves eat the ones with matchstick legs

whose is this naked body within my nakedness asks the earth
who put a glowing coal at the intersection of the snow and my
    knees
why does the cock of heather call his petals his crest

and why does the beggar on the square open his fly for a few
    pennies' alms

< 89 >

Odeur de cendre tiède et de femme accroupie
celle qui touille les braises comme soupe de pauvre dissout du
    revers de sa louche peur et grumeaux

l'arbre adossé à sa fenêtre compte dans les deux sens les morts
    alignés devant sa haie
ils sont vingt puisqu'ils ne sont que dix
à réclamer leur paye à la femme qui discute à perdre haleine avec
    son feu

< 90 >

Odor of warm ashes and crouching woman
she who stirs the coals like a pauper's soup dissolves fear and lumps
    with the back of her ladle

the tree leaning on her window counts the dead lined up against
    the hedge in both directions
there are twenty because there are only ten
there to claim their wages from the woman who argues with her
    fire till she's out of breath

< 91 >

Son feu n'a pas de toit
ses flammes n'ont pas de jupe
la bassine sur sa terrasse recueille le sang noir des étoiles égorgées
sa voix est rouge par temps de compromissions et de tempêtes
grise lorsqu'elle appelle les enfants qu'elle n'a pas eus
elle leur apprend les petits pois de l'addition
les cerises de l'alphabet
les bonbons acidulés de la grammaire
à se méfier du brouillard qui ne salue pas les paillassons
de l'air silence en mouvement
de l'eau souterraine
sueur secrète de la terre étalée au grand jour

< 92 >

Her fire has no roof
her flames have no skirt
the basin on her terrace catches black blood from the cut throats
    of stars
her voice is red in times of compromise and storms
gray when she calls the children she did not have
she teaches them the green peas of addition
the cherries of the alphabet
the hard candies of grammar
to beware of fog that does not greet the doormat
of air which is silence in movement
of subterranean water
secret sweat of the earth laid out in broad daylight

< 93 >

Deux lunes comme deux femmes d'un même village
font halte dans notre vestibule
elles connaissent notre miroir de réputation

Nous devons lire leurs intentions dans la flaque de lumière sur le
    dallage de la cuisine
comprendre leur présence chez nous alors que nos voisins les
    harcèlent de leurs vœux

Elles sont deux comme les sourcils d'un même visage
deux gardiennes des marées qui
frappent nos murs à chaque équinoxe
et font saigner notre mère et le grenadier

< 94 >

Two moons like two women from the same village
stop in our hallway
they know our mirror by reputation

We must read their intentions in the puddle of light on the kitchen
    tiles
understand their presence in our home while the neighbors harass
    them with greetings

There are two of them like the eyebrows on one face
two guardians of the tides who
knock on our walls at every equinox
and make our mother and the pomegranate tree bleed

< 95 >

Elle dit
il y a des voyages plus longs que les chemins
des sentiers étrécis aux dimensions des pieds
seuls les ânes savent lire la carte du pays

elle dit mais s'arrête à la seule vue d'une flaque d'eau alors qu'elle
    n'a jamais fait naufrage
à la seule vue d'un sillon alors qu'elle n'a jamais soulevé la moindre
    motte de terre
ni enterré un hanneton

< 96 >

She says
there are journeys longer than roads
paths shrunk to a foot's width
only donkeys know how to read the map of the country

she says but stops at the mere sight of a puddle of water though
    she has never been shipwrecked
at the mere sight of a furrow though she has never dug the
    smallest clod of earth
nor buried so much as a beetle

< 97 >

Elle court plus vite que le fleuve pour le surprendre à son arrivée à
    l'estuaire
lui glisse sous l'aisselle une branche d'eucalyptus contre la toux
et trois pièces en étain qui deviendront de l'or au contact du
    couchant

Elle lui crie entre deux vagues le nom de celui qui l'accueillera de
    l'autre côté de l'horizon
reconnaissable à la fleur blanche derrière l'oreille
et cette manière de s'asseoir sur la mer comme au bord d'un
    chemin

< 98 >

She runs more swiftly than the river to surprise it when it arrives at
the estuary
slips a eucalyptus branch under its armpit to cure a cough
and three tin coins which will turn to gold on touching the sunset

Between two waves she cries out to the river the name of the one
who'll welcome it on the other side of the horizon
recognizable by a white flower behind one ear
and that way of sitting down on the sea as if by a roadside

< 99 >

Ses rêves suivent la trajectoire de la pluie
elle rêve qu'elle fait un rêve
la foule jouant aux cartes dans son miroir lui tourne le dos

moins endormie
elle les aurait chassés hors du cadre
mis en garde la dame de pique assise sur la paume du tricheur
elle aurait plié son lit devenu inutile
roi reines et valets couchant tête-bêche sur l'air

Demain
elle écrira une lettre à la tempête
exigera une comptabilité exacte des mouvements du vent
demain elle aura cent ans à cause du décalage horaire
mourra sans avoir secoué l'as de pique
pour entendre rire ses grelots

demain quand l'eau montera dans son miroir elle
demandera un sursis à la pluie pour qu'il fasse moins noir autour
    de son visage
évacuera les joueurs dans l'ordre
puis leur demandera
savez-vous au moins comment je m'appelle

< 100 >

Her dreams follow the rain's trajectory
she dreams that she had a dream
the crowd playing cards in her mirror turned its back on her

less asleep
she would have driven them from the frame
warned the queen of spades seated on the cheater's palm
she would have folded up her now-useless bed
king queens and jacks lying head-to-foot on only air

Tomorrow
she will write a letter to the storm
will demand an exact account of the wind's movements
tomorrow she will be a hundred years old because of the time
    difference
will die without having shaken the ace of spades
to hear the laughter of its bells

tomorrow when the water rises in her mirror she
will ask the rain for a reprieve so there will be less darkness around
    her face
will make the days leave in order
and then ask them
at least do you know my name

< 101 >

C'est dans son livre qu'elle ramasse les pierres qui feront fuir les
    renards
entrer deux lignes qu'elle tend son hamac
les pages tournées claquent comme linge sur une corde

son doigt sur un mot immobilise toute une foule et bloque la
    circulation de l'air
elle a de quoi rêver
mais pas de quoi vivre
toute page entre ses mains se transforme en cerf-volant

< 102 >

It's in her book that she gathers stones to chase away the foxes
she hangs her hammock between two lines
the turned pages flap like laundry on a line

her finger placed on a word immobilizes a crowd and causes a
    traffic-jam in the air
she has something to dream on
but not to live on
in her hands every page becomes a kite

< 103 >

à Marie-France Borot

Elle parle une langue blanche repêchée des eaux
nomme sept objets contondants
sept outils admis par le feu
sept herbes pour nourrir un mort familier

la neige coupée avec sa serpe
elle mange une terre si froide que ses dents deviennent diaphanes
sa main en visière sur le front
elle croit voir une hirondelle
alors qu'il s'agit d'une pierre gelée tombant à pieds joints

elle accuse à tort la configuration des murs
alors que le soleil qui lui tient d'horloge a perdu son cerceau

< 104 >

For Marie-France Borot

She speaks a white language fished up from the waters
names seven blunt objects
seven tools let in by the fire
seven grasses to feed a dead man in the family

having cut the snow with her billhook
she eats earth so cold her teeth turn transparent
using her hand as an eyeshade
she thinks she can see a swallow
but it's a frozen stone dropping with its feet together

she accuses the layout of the walls unjustly
while the sun which serves as a clock has lost its hoop

< 105 >

Elle ouvre le crépuscule à celui qui l'appelle
«mon sablier d'amour
ma bassine de frissons
mon Aladine»
mais le referme lorsqu'il jette son dévolu sur les flammes qui
    brûlent pour d'obscures raisons dans le ventre de l'âtre
alors que le vrai feu est ailleurs
dû à un bris de verres dans le miroir meublé d'un lit affable
qui s'allonge sans faire le tri entre amants de passage
et ceux qui ont traversé l'océan avec leurs charges de baisers

< 106 >

She opens the dusk to the one she calls
"my hourglass of love
my bowl of shivers
my Aladdin"
but closes it as soon as he sets his cap for the flames which burn for
    unknown reasons in the belly of the hearth
while the real fire is elsewhere
due to a shard of glass in the mirror furnished with a friendly bed
which stretches out just as gladly for casual lovers
as those who crossed an ocean with their cargo of kisses

< 107 >

Deux feuilles de menthe pour les yeux
deux grains de café pour les seins
deux pétales pour la bouche
il les abrite entre ses murs
en fait une femme au foyer
lui dessine un feu à l'intersection des branches
un rien de neige pour blanchir les cheveux de l'hiver
lui précise sa position par rapport à l'est à l'ouest
et au vent qui poussera des hommes vers sa porte

«Voilà ma femme» leur dira-t-il
froissable par temps de manque et d'humidité

< 108 >

Two mint leaves for the eyes
two coffee beans for the breasts
two petals for the mouth
he shelters them within his walls
and makes a housewife of them
draws her a fire at the branches' intersection
a bit of snow to bleach the winter's hair
makes clear to her his position on the east and the west
and on the wind which will blow men to her door

"Here is my wife," he will say to them
"who wrinkles in times of need and wet weather"

< 109 >

Le vent ne sert qu'à ébouriffer le genêt
à donner la chair de poule au renard
avec lui il faut consentir comme avec le diable

Elle n'eut pas d'enfants pour ne pas engendrer des morts
pas d'arbre pour ne pas s'encombrer de son ombre
ni de murs l'argile qu'elle pétrissait donnait un pain friable apprécié
    des serpents

elle n'eut pas de chemin non plus
son ruisseau s'était tailladé les veines de chagrins entassés
et la Grande Ourse n'était pas praticable au mois d'août

dans sa bassine de cuivre ses confitures bouillaient avec les étoiles

< 110 >

The wind is only good for tousling the broom-bush
and giving the fox gooseflesh
one must cede to it as to the devil

She had no children so as not to engender corpses
no tree so as not to burden herself with its shadow
and no walls the clay she kneaded made a crumbly bread which
    snakes appreciated

she had no road either
her stream had slashed its veins with stacked-up grief
and the Great Bear is not feasible in August

in her copper bowl jam boiled with stars

< 111 >

Le feu ne fait que s'enrichir depuis qu'on a tué le froid
il fait trois repas par jour
fait main basse sur tous les poulaillers
mange les nuages en friche les terres suspendues même le linge sur
      les cordes
les champs pauvres qu'il poursuit se jettent dans la rivière
les fleuves brûlés se roulent dans la terre
les oiseaux transformés en flammèches continuent à voler

seule Ouarda la torride n'est pas concernée
sa jument noire est devenue rousse
léchées par la langue des flammes ses roses se disent inondées de
      plaisir

< 112 >

The fire gets richer and richer since they killed the cold
it eats three meals a day
takes what it wants from the chicken coops
eats the fallow clouds and land hung like laundry on lines
poor fields fleeing it throw themselves into streams
burning rivers roll in the dust
birds turned into sparks continue flying

Only torrid Ouarda doesn't care
her black mare has become a roan
licked by the flames' tongues her roses say they're drowning in
    pleasure

< 113 >

Les enfants éphémères sortent du même trou que le perce-neige
deviennent écharde dans le cœur de l'hiver

ceux qui les croisent sur l'itinéraire des cigognes
attachent à leur cou le nom d'un arbre maternel
et une amulette pour la traversée de la forêt
qui mange les enfants oublieux

< 114 >

Transient children emerge from the same hole as the snowdrops
become splinters in the heart of winter

those who encounter them on the storks' route
tie the name of a maternal tree around their necks
and an amulet for crossing the forest
which eats forgetful children

< 115 >

La mère à leur naissance les noie avec les chats
ils s'essorent dans les deux sens
deviennent balai pinceau à trois poils plumeau
balaient les bouts de fil tombés de la robe maternelle
qui tricote des manteaux trop étroits pour des adultes
trop longs pour des nouveau-nés
se terminant toujours par une queue

Le miroir par temps de pluie sèche et de suspicion provoque
    des apparitions de loups vêtus de longs manteaux paradant
    à l'intérieur du cadre

< 116 >

Their mother drowns them at birth with the cats
they dry themselves off in both directions
become broom, three-haired paintbrush, feather duster
sweep the bits of thread fallen from the dress of their mother
who is knitting coats too narrow for adults
too long for newborns
which always end in a tail

In seasons of dry rain and suspicion the mirror teases out visions
of wolves dressed in long coats strutting inside its frame

< 117 >

Elle transforme les mots en objets
pour les toucher
les dépoussiérer
les placer à côté du chat qui préfère les souris à l'arithmétique

elle les fait cuire entre deux pierres en temps de disette
en retenant les flammes capables de divulguer leur secret

une pincée de laurier pour élever leur sens
et faire léviter la pensée tel derviche tourneur venu d'Anatolie

< 118 >

She transforms words into objects
to touch them
dust them
and place them beside the cat who prefers mice to arithmetic

She cooks them between two stones in lean times
holding back the flames which could divulge their secret

a pinch of laurel to rouse their senses
and make thought levitate like a whirling dervish from Anatolia

< 119 >

Dans quel sens tourne la terre?
demande le soleil qui se lèvera le moment venu
sans craquer la moindre allumette

Interdiction formelle de faire du feu par temps d'orage
les livres s'enflamment pour des idées
les pages qui les répètent sans comprendre sont perchoirs pour
    perroquets

Combien faut-il de jours pour atteindre la nuit?
s'impatiente la lune

< 120 >

In what direction does the earth turn?
asks the sun which will rise at the right moment
without striking any match

It is forbidden to light fires in stormy weather
books flare up for ideas
the pages which repeat them without understanding are parrots'
    perches

How many days does it take to reach night?
the moon asks impatiently

< 121 >

Quand tout s'éteint
que les ombres glissent des murs et s'aplatissent le long des
    plinthes
il y a ces feuilles mortes qui marchent sur les vitres
leurs paumes tournées vers l'intérieur

La fillette qui a troué la nuit de son doigt translucide
les prend pour des mariés et leur jette des poignées de riz
qui retombent du côté opposé à la pluie
tricotant un habit chaud pour le jardin si pauvre

< 122 >

When everything fades away
and shadows slide from the walls and flatten themselves against the
    baseboard
there are dead leaves which walk along the panes
their palms turned towards the interior

The little girl who made a hole in the night with her translucent
    finger
mistakes them for brides and grooms and throws rice at them
which falls on the side opposite the rain
and knits warm clothes for the impoverished garden

Ils sont deux figuiers à manger leurs fruits dans l'obscurité
à lancer les épluchure sur les vitres
celui qui a vue sur l'âtre raconte les colères des flammes
l'aveuglement de la suie
l'obstination de la marmite et de la femme à se vêtir de deuil
Ils la croient partie avec le chemin quand sa robe n'héberge que le
    vent
sa nudité taillée dans une lumière pauvre les rassure
le duvet dans ses creux les déconcerte
il provient du ventre du gallinacé tournant dans sa mort

< 124 >

There are two fig trees eating their fruit in the darkness
throwing the peels against the windowpanes
the one that saw the hearth tells about the flames' anger
the soot's blindness
the pot's and the woman's insistence on wearing mourning
They thought she had left with the road when her dress sheltered
    only wind
her nakedness cut from a dim light reassures them
the down in her hollows disturbs them
it comes from the belly of the hen turning round in its death

< 125 >

Elle loue la soupente à des chats revêches qui entretiennent des
    rapports affables avec les pigeons
son papier peint au mur jaunit au même rythme que l'ellébore du
    jardin

Elle trouve mauvaise mine au saint suspendu derrière la porte
souffreteuse est son image dans le miroir
ses aisselles sentent le mégot de cigarette

Loin le temps où il pesait son poids de cierges et de génuflexions
le village depuis la dernière pluie a rompu sa laisse
l'arc-en-ciel a bu l'eau du bénitier

< 126 >

She rents the attic to surly cats who are on good terms with the
    pigeons
her wallpaper yellows along with the hellebore in the garden

She thinks that the saint hung behind the door doesn't look at all
    well
his reflection in the mirror is sickly
his armpits smell of cigarette butts

Long gone now is the time when he was worth his weight in
    candles and genuflections
since the last rain the village broke from its leash
the rainbow drank the holy water from the font

< 127 >

Maison sans devant
sans arrière
le vent traité en mendiant n'aime ni la femme ni sa haie

il a cabossé le ventre de sa marmite
cassé l'oreille de sa jarre
accroché au caroubier la laine noire de sa quenouille
les veines de ses mains terminent leur parcours sous les ongles
devenus écorces
silex incisant les murs jusqu'au sang lorsqu'un pas s'approche de la
    porte sans s'arrêter

< 128 >

House with no front
and no back
the wind that was treated like a beggar likes neither the woman
    nor her hedge

it dented the belly of her stew pot
broke her pitcher's spout
tied the black wool from its distaff to the carob tree
the veins of its hands end their journey beneath fingernails turned
    to bark
flintstone cutting the walls till they bleed when footsteps approach
    her door and don't stop

< 129 >

Troc aux portes des faubourgs
les gens d'en haut venus se ravitailler en bruits
échangent un âne contre une horloge
un ruisseau contre un miroir de poche
un bénitier contre un seau en plastique
des flocons de neige contre un oreiller
trois plumes de coq contre un bicorne
une famille de genêt contre un annuaire du téléphone
Seuls les morts ne trouvent pas preneur
assis à l'écart
ils attendent la fin des marchandages pour rentrer chez eux à pied

< 130 >

Barter where the city meets the suburbs
the upper crust come to stock up on noises
exchange a donkey for a clock
a stream for a pocket mirror
a holy water font for a plastic bucket
a few snowflakes for a pillow
three cock feathers for a cocked hat
a family of broom-bushes for a telephone directory
Only the dead find no takers
seated in the background
they wait for the bargaining to be over to go home on foot

< 131 >

Lune voilée de septembre fait baisser les jupes des filles
le coquelicot est tache de sang sur le genou de l'été
le travailleur saisonnier s'appuie sur sa serpe et oublie de respirer
son désir égrené tinte comme chapelet de croyant
il prie le dieu de la nuit d'écourter le jour

< 132 >

September's veiled moon lowers girls' hemlines
poppies are a bloodstain on summer's knee
the migrant worker leans on his scythe and forgets to breathe
his desires plucked from the branch click like rosary beads
he prays to the god of night to shorten the day

< 133 >

Lune sous la table ronronne avec le chat
la femme qui noue laine et rayons
lui tisse un tapis de prières à quatre nœuds

Elle a des chagrins gros comme des moineaux
quand le soleil rebrousse chemin au-dessus de son pommier
le cercle de feu n'a jamais tiré l'eau de son puits
tiré la charrue de son bœuf
ou soufflé sa bougie quand les coyotes par temps de neiges sourdes
    encerclent sa maison

< 134 >

Moon under the table purrs with the cat
the woman who knots yarn and rays together
weaves it a four-knotted prayer rug

She has sorrows the size of sparrows
when the sun retraces its steps above her apple tree
the fiery circle has never drawn water from her well
pulled the plow for her ox
or blown out the candle when, in seasons of deaf snow, coyotes
    encircle her house

< 135 >

Lune grosse de deux marées a des nausées
l'odeur des algues fait tourner son lait
son désir de maternité remonte à la première caverne
quand lunes et cailloux s'étripaient pour un silex

le soleil à l'époque était un cercle vide
cerceau pour apprendre à sauter aux jeunes rayons
roue de brouette pour transporter les vieilles comètes
houppette pour poudrer le nez d'étoiles atteintes de strabisme
à force de loucher vers la Voie lactée

< 136 >

Moon big with two tides has fits of nausea
the odor of algae turns its milk
its desire for motherhood goes back to the first cave
when moons and pebbles battled over a flint

the sun at that time was an empty circle
a hoop to teach the young rays how to jump
wheel of a barrow to carry old comets
puff to powder the noses of stars gone cross-eyed
from ogling the Milky Way

< 137 >

Lune basse de septembre arrondit l'angle des maisons
et prend dans le même cercle âne et fauvette
le cœur du facteur grince à sa vue dans les montées
sa sacoche perd un vœu à chaque tournant
sa bicyclette morte tournera à vide dans le paradis des postiers
le courrier en souffrance émettra un son plaintif chaque fois qu'un
    mot d'amour frôlera son écho

< 138 >

Low September moon rounds off the houses' corners
and catches the donkey and the warbler in the same circle
the mailman's heart creaks when he sees it as he climbs
his mailbag loses a vow at every turning
his dead bicycle's wheels will turn uselessly in postmen's paradise
rerouted letters will emit a plaintive noise each time a love-word
    grazes their echo

< 139 >

«Lune pieuse en route pour La Mecque attrape fou rire à chaque
    secousse du chameau»

Les femmes qui la pourchassent de leurs vœux la dessinent sur leur
    paume
assise sur un ballot de cumin

Le désert est sa résidence principale
le Tibet son lieu de villégiature
les moines ses fournisseurs en incantations

C'est elle qui blanchit les osselets
elle qui fait tourner les moulins à prière

< 140 >

"Pious moon on its way to Mecca bursts out laughing at the
     camel's every jolt "

The women who pursue the moon with their vows draw it on
     their palms
seated on a bundle of cumin

The desert is its principle residence
it spends its holidays in Tibet
monks supply it with incantations

It's the moon which whitens jacks and knucklebones
and turns the prayer mills

< 141 >

Elle réalisa que la maison était morte quand les murs se mirent à
    brouter la haie
d'ailleurs la maison n'était pas une maison
mais une succession d'opacités et de transparences

Le cimetière non plus n'était pas un cimetière
mais lieu de passage des regrets
convoyeur des suppliques bues par les pierres
le deuil grandissait ceux qui le traversaient sans renverser les stèles

Tombes aménagées comme chambres de poupées
sauter à pieds joints faisait partie des réjouissances
les défunts imitaient le merle

La femme qui suivait l'arbre avait les aisselles vertes
l'ourlet défait d'une branche la fit trébucher
la hache sous sa jupe coupait l'eau le feu pas la douleur

< 142 >

She realized that the house was dead when the walls began to
    graze on the hedge
besides the house wasn't really a house
but a succession of opacities and transparencies

The cemetery wasn't a cemetery either
but a passageway for regrets
an escort for petitions drunk by the rocks
mourning exalted those who crossed it without knocking over any
    tombstones

Graves fitted out like rooms in dolls' houses
jumping into them is part of the festivities
the dead imitate the blackbird

The woman who followed the tree had green armpits
the undone hem of a branch made her stumble
the hatchet beneath her skirt cut water fire not grief

< 143 >

Elle applique ses mains sur celles du pommier pour vérifier sa
     résistance au chagrin
elle se sent responsable des blessures de ses genoux
et des sept lieues qu'il parcourut à pied pour se fixer face à sa porte

elle lui apprit les vingt et une manières de marcher contre le vent
et comment se lever avant la lampe sans l'offenser

Il observa un mutisme douloureux devant la première neige et le
     premier cheveu blanc de la femme
convaincu que Dieu gaspillait sa réserve de craie

< 144 >

She lays her hands on the apple tree's hands to test its resistance to
  grief
she feels responsible for the wounds on its knees
and the seven leagues it had to come on foot to root itself facing
  her door

she taught it the twenty-one ways of walking against the wind
and how to get up before the lamp without hurting its feelings

The tree stayed sorrowfully silent observing the first snow and the
  woman's first white hair
convinced that God was wasting his supply of chalk

< 145 >

La carte de géographie du pays était trouée entre nord et sud
le facteur distribuait des lettres sans nouvelles
un botaniste se suicida pour une jonquille
elle avait oublié son nom

Seuls les renards avaient des réminiscences
absents du registre de la mairie
poules et coqs étaient consignés dans leur carnet

dans quelle main est ma main demandait l'amoureuse
vois-tu nos cœurs dans le miroir
pourquoi fait-il si noir sous ma robe?

< 146 >

The map of the country was slashed from north to south
the postman delivered letters with no news
a botanist killed himself over a daffodil
that had forgotten his name

Only the foxes remembered anything
although absent from the town hall registry
hens and cocks were listed in their notebooks

in whose hand is my hand asked the woman in love
do you see our hearts in the mirror
why is it so dark under my dress?

< 147 >

Sa conviction que la mort sortira de son miroir
de la paume de sa main
ou même de l'écorce du tilleul qu'elle a omis d'élaguer
elle fera le siège d'objets transis
assiettes ébréchées
théière refroidie
drap plié à l'envers
sa certitude que le parquet criera pour elle
que les volets grinceront des dents
qu'elle sera enterrée dans l'épaisseur du tain
sans avoir soulagé le tilleul qui regarde ailleurs pour échapper à la
    vue de la morte qui vieillit dans un miroir

< 148 >

Her belief that death will emerge from her mirror
or from the palm of her hand
or even from the bark of the lime tree she neglected to prune
she will lay siege to transfixed things:
chipped plates
cold teapot
sheet folded inside-out
her certainty that the parquet will cry out for her
that the shutters will gnash their teeth
that she will be buried in the mirror's silvering
without having comforted the lime tree which will look elsewhere
    to escape the gaze of the dead woman aging in her mirror

< 149 >

Un homme habite sa maison
sept soleils mangent dans son assiette
ses abeilles sont assez grandes pour se rendre au champ
elle a de quoi parader et se nourrir
mais pas de quoi rire
sa marmite a de gros chagrins de suie

< 150 >

A man lives in her house
seven suns eat from her plate
seven bees are big enough to go out to the fields
she has enough to show off about and enough to eat
but nothing to laugh at
her stew pot is having a fit of soot

< 151 >

Elle ne balaie plus devant sa porte
ne se dispute plus avec le vent qui ébouriffe son faux poivrier
elle lit la pluie dans le désordre
apprend que mars vole son encre à décembre
et deux jours au plumier de février

sa lampe s'interdit de dormir l'hiver quand les livres se prennent
    pour des oreillers
que les lucioles font un feu d'ailes pour réchauffer les choses
    transies:
lits à une place
lettres de rupture
et ces disparues qui traversent impassibles les pièces dans un
    froissement d'étoffes

< 152 >

She doesn't sweep in front of her door anymore
no longer argues with the wind which tousles her false pepper tree
she reads the rain in her disorder
learns that March stole December's ink
and two days from February's pencil-case

her lamp won't let itself sleep in winter when the books think that
      they're pillows
when fireflies make a pyre of their wings to warm up chilled things:
single beds
Dear John letters
and those departed women who cross rooms imperturbably with a
      rustling of cloth

< 153 >

Quelqu'un frappe à sa vitre et lui fait signe de le suivre
elle réalise qu'elle est morte et s'en attriste

Dans quel sens tourner autour de mon corps demande-t-elle au
    moulin à café
dans quelle poche ai-je rangé mes larmes
à quel orphelinat confier mes abeilles
pourquoi la cascade gelée me tire-t-elle la langue
pour quelles raisons suis-je incapable de parler avec mon livre

< 154 >

Someone raps on her windowpane and signals her to follow
she realizes she is dead, which saddens her

in which direction should I go around my body she asks the coffee
    mill
in which pocket did I put my tears
in which orphanage shall I leave my bees
why does the frozen waterfall tug at my tongue
why am I no longer able to talk to my book?

< 155 >

Bulbes plantés à l'envers fleuriront la maison du diable
et l'ellébore stérile n'a qu'à se laisser saillir ventre béant sous les
    coups de boutoir du vent

La femme ouverte sur les jardins
exhorte le voyageur de laisser la pluie derrière lui
il n'a rien à craindre des murs
rien à craindre de la poussette
envolée depuis que l'enfant s'est endormi

< 156 >

Bulbs planted upside down decorate the devil's house with flowers
and the sterile hellebore need only thrust out its open womb to the
  wind's attack

The woman open on the gardens
urges the traveler to leave the rain behind him
he has nothing to fear from the walls
nothing to fear from the stroller
which flew off as soon as the child went to sleep

< 157 >

Un arbre rouge pour celle riche d'un jardin fendu en terre
    palpitante
le fruit égrené sur ses seins étourdit les abeilles
Elle lève une armée de pluies contre les tourterelles qui piétinent
    son allée
encercle son puits d'herbe chauffée à blanc par celui qui souffle le
    chaud et le froid dans ses cavités
le cuivre du soleil doit sa longévité à son coup de marteau

< 158 >

A red tree for the woman whose wealth is a slit garden of pulsing
    earth
the peeled fruit on her breasts stuns the bees
She raises an army of rain against the doves who trample her lane
surrounds her well with grass made white-hot by the one who
    blows hot and cold in her cavities
the sun's copper owes its longevity to his hammer-blow

< 159 >

Mourir donne l'impression de courir
dit-elle
on troue un brouillard
on enjambe un mur sans l'effleurer par respect du liseron
on se précipite dans toutes les directions
on croise des silhouettes sorties des vieux livres:
un philosophe
un prophète
un enfant
qui effeuillent la même page
mâchent la même phrase
remâchée par un cheval
puis par un âne qui n'aime pas le cheval

Derrière le dos du philosophe du prophète de l'enfant de l'âne et
    du cheval
des anges brûlent leurs ailes pour se réchauffer

Mourir ce n'est donc que cela
se dit-elle en tournant la page de son sommeil

< 160 >

Dying makes you feel as if you're running
she says
you make a hole in the fog
step over a wall without grazing it out of respect for the bindweed
you rush in every direction
encounter figures out of old books:
a philosopher
a prophet
a child
who pull the petals from the same page
chew on the same sentence
grazed on by a horse
then by an ass who doesn't like the horse

Behind the backs of the philosopher the prophet the child the ass
    and the horse
angels burn their wings to warm themselves

So dying is nothing more than that
she says to herself while turning the page of her sleep

< 161 >

La dernière marche est celle du souffle retenu
du corps répudié
on campe dans l'attente
le goutte-à-goutte des bruits est traduit en appels

La ménagère rapièce des mots déchirés
un faiseur fait s'entrechoquer des phrases sans produire la moindre
    étincelle
un nostalgique donnerait sa vie pour un trille
«La mer a envahi toutes les maisons» annonce un retardataire
mais personne ne le croit

Ils ont trop à faire pour vider la terre de sa mauvaise terre
le monde qui leur tourne le dos n'est visible qu'à hauteur d'enfant

< 162 >

The last step is the held breath
of the repudiated body
we camp out in expectation
the dripping of noise becomes a call to arms

The housewife mends torn words
a craftsman rubs sentences together without producing the
    slightest spark
someone nostalgic would give his life for a trill
"The sea has invaded all the houses" announces a latecomer
but no one believes him

They have too much work to do weeding the earth
the world which turns its back on them is only visible from a
    child's height

< 163 >

«Il n'y a pas trois jours sans pluie
ni trois arpents de terre sans ruisseau»

Blanche comme laine cardée la voix de celle qui remplace les objets
    perdus par des objets perdus
le sel dévoreur de neige la fait réfléchir
elle essaie de comprendre où commence la terre
où finit le chagrin
et pourquoi l'homme qui mangea du foin mordit un loup

< 164 >

"There are never three days without rain
nor three acres of land without a stream"

White as carded wool is the voice of the woman who replaces lost
    objects with lost objects
the snow-devouring salt makes her think
she tries to understand where the earth begins
where grief ends
and why the man who ate hay bit a wolf

< 165 >

Nuit suspendue dans le vide
accrochée aux rebords des balcons
assise au chevet d'un mur éboulé

les jardiniers soignent les insomnies de la passiflore
les chats crient leur désir dans les gouttières de février

«Ne m'oublie pas lui crie la lune
j'habite une ville où les rues ne mènent jamais à des maisons»

< 166 >

Night suspended in the void
hung from the ledges of balconies
seated at a crumbling wall's bedside

gardeners nurse the passionflowers' insomnia
cats yowl their desire in February's gutters

"Don't forget me," the moon cries to it
"I live in a town where the streets never lead to houses"

< 167 >

Maison
sans murs sans fenêtres
la lune à califourchon sur le toit tombe d'étonnement dans le puits
la femme qui la repêche avec une épuisette
l'essore
la défroisse
la sèche sur sa corde
puis la rend à son destin attachée à un ballon

«Reviens me voir lui crie-t-elle
de préférence un jour hors des jours et de l'année»

< 168 >

House
without walls without windows
the moon seated cross-legged on the roof falls into the well in
    astonishment
the woman who fishes it out with a shrimp-net
wrings it out
smooths its wrinkles
dries it on her clothesline
then sends it back to its fate attached to a balloon

"Come back to see me" she calls to it
"some day not on the calendar would be best"

< 169 >

La pluie venue de l'autre versant a rétréci son champ
on dirait un mouchoir trop lavé
et ce n'est pas sa gouttière qui empêchera sa maison de glisser dans
    le ravin
la montagne qui a ses soucis ne peut tout gérer
les empoignades entre vents et épineux ensanglantent la pente
ameutent les cailloux médisants

< 170 >

The rain come from the other side of the hill has shrunk its field
it looks like a handkerchief washed over and over again
and it's not the drainpipe which will keep the house from sliding
    into the ravine
the mountain which has its own problems can't tend to everything
brawls between winds and thorn bushes have bloodied the slope
and attracted a crowd of gossip-mongering pebbles

< 171 >

Elle a la voix du frêne dans le vent
elle est mère de sept filles qui vont de sa huche jusqu'aux orteils du
    pommier
elle n'épousa personne mais fut veuve de tous les arbres de la forêt
elle n'a ni voisins ni vœux à formuler mais une aiguille pour
    coudre ses murs fissurés par les regards envieux

d'une liaison sans lendemain avec un résineux
elle eut un fils
un vrai tournesol au soleil

< 172 >

She has the voice of an ash tree in the wind
she is mother to seven daughters who go from her bread box to
    the apple tree's toes
she married no one but was the widow of all the trees in the forest
she has neither neighbors nor vows to pronounce, only a needle to
    sew up her walls cracked by jealous glances

from a one-night stand with a thorn bush
she had a son
a real sunflower in the daylight

< 173 >

Dans le même trou
le bébé mort les larmes du cerisier et l'alphabet
il a toute l'éternité pour apprendre à lire
«Pleure-toi un peu» lui crie un merle
tu marcheras à la Toussaint
quand il te poussera des ailes

< 174 >

Down in the same hole
the dead baby the cherry tree's tears and the alphabet
he has all eternity to learn to read
"Cry a little," a blackbird calls out to him
"you'll walk on All Souls' Day
when you grow wings"

< 175 >

Il est des funérailles conviviales
comme jour de battage du blé sur l'aire
quand les bœufs tournent en cercles serrés pour retenir l'âme du
    grain

La femme acheminée vers la terre éventrée
faisait un pain de la taille de la lune
puis l'incisait du revers de la main

même croix sur la huche et le couvercle de sapin
un soleil mauvais a abaissé la pâte
et brouillé le teint de l'œillet

< 176 >

There are convivial funerals
like the day of threshing wheat on the threshing floor
when the oxen go around in tight circles to hold in the soul of the
    grain

The woman being relocated to the eviscerated land
made a loaf of bread the size of the moon
then cut into it with the back of her hand

the same cross on the bread box and the pine lid
a bad sun has let the crust fall
and clouded the carnation's complexion

< 177 >

Les fleuves qui coulent à plat ventre sont des chevaux abandonnés
la vue d'une robe sur une corde les rend nostalgiques
la croupe du buis leur rappelle une jument consentante

Ils ferment les yeux lorsqu'un peuplier en rut s'essuie sur leur
    berge
s'attristent quand une lavandière essore son linge de travers

Ils suivent les enterrements à distance
sûrs de croiser à l'embouchure l'âme du défunt

< 178 >

Rivers that run with their bellies to the ground are abandoned
    horses
the sight of a dress on a clothesline makes them nostalgic
a boxwood tree's rump reminds them of a willing mare

They close their eyes when a poplar in heat dries off on their banks
are saddened when a laundress wrings her clothes inside out

They follow burials at a distance
sure of meeting the dead man's soul at the estuary

< 179 >

Personne ici ne relève les maisons écroulées
personne n'essore les jardins inondés

On fraternise avec un arbre de passage
on hume à distance les filles trémières et les épouses épicées
on se méfie de la femme qui n'a pas de bâton pour attraper la
    volaille
ni de hachoir pour casser ses os
ni de marmite pour nourrir l'étranger

Celui qui meurt adossé à l'arbre appartient à l'arbre
à la galaxie qui clignote sous ses paupières cousues par une grande
    fatigue

< 180 >

No one here helps fallen houses to get up
no one wrings out flooded gardens

They fraternize with a passing tree
sniff at a distance hollyhock girls and spicy wives
they mistrust the woman with no stick to catch a chicken
nor hatchet to break its bones
nor stew pot to feed the stranger

He who dies with his back against a tree belongs to the tree
to the galaxy that blinks beneath his eyelids sewn shut by great
    weariness

< 181 >

LES MARINS SANS NAVIRE

< 182 >

THE SAILORS WITHOUT A SHIP

à Marie-Laure de Villepin

Elle attend à sa fenêtre la mer avec sa horde de marins pour l'aider
    à gauler son noyer

Jadis elle possédait une maison avec sa parcelle d'océan
un toit avec son pesant de vent
les mouettes remplaçaient le chien

elle attribuait à une illusion d'optique l'intrusion des vagues dans
    sa chambre
s'endormait pendant que l'eau montait
son vacarme contenait le silence des navires sans attaches
devenus muets depuis que l'océan s'est ensablé

< 184 >

For Marie-Laure de Villepin

She waits at her window for the sea with its crowd of sailors to
    help her beat down the fruit from the walnut tree

A long time ago
she owned a house with its plot of ocean
a roof with its share of wind
there were seagulls instead of a dog

She assumed the intrusion of waves in her bedroom was an optical
    illusion
went to sleep as the water rose
their din contained the sorrowful silence of unmoored boats
become mute since the ocean filled with sand

< 185 >

La mer qui voyage sans relâche vieillit plus vite que les phares
les décalages horaires blanchissent les cheveux des vagues
les marins bigleux les prennent pour des écheveaux de laine
et rêvent de manteaux tricotés main

Ils disent les glaciers sans cœur alors qu'ils fondent à la seule vue
    d'une pâquerette

< 186 >

The sea that travels unceasingly ages faster than the lighthouses
the waves' hair has gone white with jet lag
nearsighted sailors mistake them for skeins of wool
and dream of hand-knitted coats

They say the glaciers are heartless, but they melt at the mere sight
of a daisy

< 187 >

Il dit avoir fait naufrage dans toutes les directions
que son navire devenu hamac se balance entre deux pôles
qu'il appela la terre
suivit un brouillard
pleura à la vue du pain

Les femmes délièrent leur ceinture pour qu'il accède à leur herbe
il sarcla
creusa des travées d'écume avec l'approbation des sillons
puis déclara:
les vrais marins naviguent avec les poissons du plaisir sur des récifs
    femelles

< 188 >

He says he was shipwrecked in every direction
that his ship, become a hammock, swung between the poles
that he called to the earth
followed a fog
wept at the sight of bread

Women undid their belts so he could get at their grass
he weeded
he dug rows of foam with the furrows' approval
then declared:
real sailors navigate with pleasure-fish on female reefs

pour Ghassan Tuéni

Les marins sans navire ont d'étranges hallucinations quand la mer
    fait son ménage saisonnier
les algues gesticulant bras nus sont des fiancées défuntes
les balançoires tendues entre les continents sont chargées de
    mouettes
et de rires d'enfants

la détresse des mousses est infinie quand ils pensent aux genoux
    écorchés des fillettes
leurs pleurs trouent les vagues
et les squales qui s'inclinent devant elles ne leur veulent pas du bien
sous leurs vestes serrées ils cachent des nageoires inamicales
et les marins qui le savent oublient d'éteindre leurs lanternes

Les marins sans navire relient le fixe au mouvant
l'opaque au transparent
l'horizon aurait tendu sa corde entre deux pommiers sans leur
    intervention
l'eau noire est leur cinquième élément
la mauvaise sueur de la terre
le sang frelaté des houillères
leur domicile fixe quand les continents cassent leur vaisselle

< 190 >

For Ghassan Tuéni

The sailors without a ship have strange hallucinations when the sea
    does its spring cleaning
The bare-armed fronds of gesticulating seaweed are dead
    sweethearts
The swings hung between the continents are filled with seagulls
    and children's laughter

The cabin boys' distress is infinite when they think of little girls'
    scraped knees
their sobs pierce the waves
and the sharks who bow before the waves don't wish them well
under their tight jackets they hide unfriendly fins
and the sailors who know it forget to put out their lanterns

The sailors without a ship link the fixed to the mobile
the opaque to the transparent
the horizon would have stretched its cord between two apple trees
    without their intervention
black water is their fifth element
the sick sweat of the earth
the watered blood of coal mines
their fixed abode when the continents smash their dishes

< 191 >

Les vieux navires craignent de mourir en montagne
entourés de loups hurlant comme corne de brume par temps de
  marée sombre et d'avarie
loin des capitaines aux yeux d'encre qui racontent leur vie un
  compas à la main
Le sel de leur barbe provient des tonneaux de saumure alignés dans
  les cales
des robes surannées des poissons femelles qui rêvent de pingouins
  endimanchés

< 192 >

The old ships are afraid of dying in the mountains
surrounded by wolves howling like foghorns in a season of dark
    tides and damage in transit
far from ink-eyed captains who tell their life stories, compass in
    hand
The salt of their beards comes from barrels of brine lined up in the
    hold
from the outdated gowns of female fish who dream of penguins in
    their Sunday best

Les enfants qui n'ont pas de père balaient les rues de leur
    fureur   ils cherchent des marins riches d'arbres à pain et
    d'océans centenaires   leurs pieds foulant les embouchures
    deviennent translucides   les orteils minuscules servent de
    phare aux navires qui sombrent
Ils jettent de la terre sur la terre avant d'embarquer   effacent
    tout ce qui n'est pas doté de parole:
maisons isolées
tombes anonymes
ruelles sans issue
les pluies méticuleuses effaceront les montagnes   laissées
    derrière eux   ils s'éloignent sur une même vague
leur sang s'épaissit à mesure que vieillit la mer

< 194 >

The fatherless children sweep the streets with their rage   they
    look for sailors with a wealth of bread trees and
    centenarian oceans   their feet trampling the river mouths
    become transparent   their tiny toes serve as lighthouses for
    sinking ships
They throw earth on the earth before embarking   erase
    everything not endowed with speech:
isolated houses
unmarked graves
dead-end streets
meticulous rains will erase the mountains   they leave behind
    them   they go away on the same wave
their blood thickens as the sea ages

< 195 >

La route qui va de Circé à la Grande Ourse passe sous sa fenêtre
les enfants l'empruntent pour se rendre à l'école
les tabliers au passage accrochent une étoile dormante
une plainte s'élève en forme d'étincelle
Bérénice la frileuse rêve d'une couette
Bételgeuse l'égarée d'un jardin clôturé d'un trèfle à quatre feuilles

Le temps est au chèvrefeuille et à la méditation
les gens marchent dans leur sommeil
les écoles suivent le vent
les enfants sont en papier

< 196 >

The road that leads from the Compass to the Great Bear passed
      under our windows
children took it to go to school
passing by, their school smocks caught on a sleeping star
a cry rose up in the form of a spark
chilly Bérénice dreamed of a quilt
and footloose Betelgeuse of an enclosed garden and a six-leafed
      clover

It was a time of honeysuckle and laziness
people walked in their sleep
schools followed the wind
the children were made of paper

< 197 >

Accroupie sur la lagune
elle hèle les choses transies rejetées par la mer
peigne en écaille
miroir à deux faces
flacon vide
et cette chaise à bascule nécessaire pour la sieste des vagues

Chaque objet ramassé l'éloigne de la terre
elle retrouvera sa maison sur l'autre rive
essorera sa robe
avant de pousser la porte

< 198 >

Crouched over the lagoon
she calls out to the pierced things rejected by the sea
tortoise-shell comb
mirror with two faces
empty perfume bottle
and that rocking chair needed for the waves' siesta

Each object gathered distances her from the earth
she will find her house on the other shore
will wring out her dress
before pushing the door open

< 199 >

L'ombre laineuse des nuages réchauffe les noyés
la vieille dame retrousse sa jupe pour laisser passer une baleine
la jeune fille se mariera dans l'année son étoile de mer au front

La mer ne peut être partout
caresser les poissons dans le sens des nageoires occupe ses mains
et les noyés aux bouches ensablées n'ont pas frappé à sa porte
n'ont pas décliné leur nom
ni celui de leur navire devenu branche morte

< 200 >

The clouds' woolly shadows warm drowned men
the old lady lifts her skirt to let a whale pass
the young girl will be married within a year with a starfish on her
    forehead

The sea can't be everywhere
stroking fish along their gills occupied its hands
and drowned men with mouths full of sand have not knocked at its
    door
nor given their names
nor that of their ship turned into a dead branch

< 201 >

Les galets
c'est des noyés devenus pierreux à force de retenir leurs larmes
la femme les aligne sur son seuil par ordre de chagrin
le chien leur apprend à courir
les feuilles du frêne à applaudir
le puits à lire dans les intentions

Elle les laisse dire lorsqu'ils prétendent descendre d'une lignée
     prestigieuse de montagnes
parler de droite à gauche comme dans les firmans anciens
ânonner l'alphabet coufique
lettres martelées tels clous sur semelle de chamelier
mais se fâche
et les traite de cailloux, d'épluchures de requins, de vomi de
     continents
lorsqu'ils prennent un palmier pour un minaret
une procession de fourmis pour une caravane
et le perroquet pour le muezzin

< 202 >

Small rocks on the beach
are drowned men turned stony from holding back their tears
the woman lines them up on her doorstep in the order of their
    grief
the dog teaches them to run
the ash leaves teach them to clap
the well, to read intentions

She lets them have their say when they claim to descend from a
    prestigious range of mountains
speak from right to left like ancient caliphs' edicts
stumble through the Coufic alphabet
hammering the letters like nails in a camel-driver's shoe
but she becomes angry
calls them pebbles, shark peelings, continents' vomit
when they mistake a palm tree for a minaret
a line of ants for a caravan
and the parrot for a muezzin

< 203 >

LES OBSCURCIS

THE DARKENED ONES

< 205 >

à Claude Esteban

1.

Nous nous sommes exclus de l'espace informe de l'air
pour une terre soucieuse de combler ses excavations avec
os   chiffons   aboiements
Nous avons perdus cette mobilité propre aux objets reconnaissables
     à leurs contours
nous nous sommes décolorés

2.

Egaux lors de la distribution des peines et pour éviter toute
     revendication
on nous serra en fagots silencieux
sans préciser à quelle forêt nous appartenions
sans accès à nos noms placés plus haut que nous
lisibles des murs dressés dur leur unique pied

3.

Les voix de la ville nous arrivent disloquées
les reconstituer en ligne droite exige le savoir faire d'un aprenteur
     de cadastre
les appels chevauchant l'écho s'allongent jusqu'aux cloisons sourdes
détissent l'air
l'accrochent en lambeaux sur les haies renversées
drap ou linceul qu'importe

4.

Donnez-moi une boîte d'alumettes où me loger
deux pétales de fleur pour me nourrir
et que le monde soit gouverné par une cigale

< 206 >

For Claude Esteban

1.

We had shut ourselves out of the air's shapeless space
for a ground eager to fill its hollows with
bones   rags   barking
we lost that mobility belonging to objects recognizable by their
    shape
we discolored ourselves

2.

Equal when tasks were assigned and to avoid any protests
we were bound up in silent firewood- bundles
without knowing to what forest we had once belonged
with no access to our names set above us
to be read by the walls, standing on their single foot

3.

The city's voices come to us mangled
untangling them into a straight line takes a land-surveyor's skill
calls astride the echo stretch out to the deaf walls
unravel the air
and hang it in strips on the overturned hedges
sheet or shroud, what's the difference

4.

Give me a matchbox to live in
two flower petals to feed myself
and let the world be ruled by a grasshopper

< 207 >

Nous glissons
glissons avec la planète
nous maigrissons pour nourrir un sol famélique de notre chair
personne n'a le bras assez long pour ouvrir aux voyageurs
    souterrains
personne n'a l'energie pour préparer la mue de trépas à vie
personne n'a localisé le passage prohibé

5.

Nous limons nos aspérités pour rassurer ceux qui nous prennent
    pour des loups
pour des instruments émettant le même son osseux
ou des caisses de clameurs alors que nous n'accusons personne de
    la restriction de nos déplacements
pataugeant sans cesse dans nos étuis
drap ou linceul qu'importe

6.

Les nostalgiques cherchent leur forme dans leurs vêtements
    évaporés
ignorant que le chagrin ne retient pas le lin
et que des jardiniers vigilants plient dans le même sens peu et
    écorce

7.

Les rêveurs attendent la saison des lucioles pour copuler
les millions de battements d'ailes limant la chair
nous nous emboitons
feignons des coîts
et que les ascètes s'enterrent de leurs propres mains
oubliant qu'ils le sont déjà et qu'il n'y a pas plus mort qu'eux

< 208 >

We were sliding
sliding with the planet
we were growing thinner to feed an earth starving for our flesh
no one has arms long enough to open the door to underground
    travelers
no one has the energy for molting from death into life
no one has found the forbidden passageway

5.

We soften our sharpnesses to reassure those who mistake us for
    wolves
for instruments emitting the same bony sound
or crates full of clamor though we hold no one responsible for
    restricting our movements
floundering endlessly in our cases
sheet or shroud, what's the difference

6.

The nostalgic seek their own shapes in evaporated garments
not knowing that grief doesn't crease linen
and that watchful gardeners fold skin and bark in the same
    direction

7.

The dreamers waited for firefly season to copulate
millions of wing-beats filing off the flesh
we fit into each other
imitated intercourse
and let the ascetics bury themselves with their own hands
forgetting that they were buried already, and no one was more
    dead than they

< 209 >

8.

Ramenés dans leur volume les fugeurs sont traités de revenants
ne disposant que du son de la lumière
de l'ombre des bruits
d'une porte dessinée

9.

Repeints à neuf
les nouveaux venus nous interrogent sur ce qu'ils ont laissé
    derrière eux
alors qu'ils devraient nous apprendre ce que nous sommes devenus
nous dire si nous sommes vagues ou précis
mouillés ou secs
ils rient de nous voir si maigres alors qu'ils perdent du poids à
    chaque inclinaison de la planète
quand le dessus devient dessous
entrainant l'horizon et le linge sur les cordes
draps ou linceuls qu'importe

10.

Ils disent des choses pensables mais que personne ne retient
sur les assiettes ébréchées et les parapluies retournés par le vent
mais font l'impasse sur novembre qui referme les portes après le
    dernier visiteur et sur les sains qui reprennent posession des
    allées

ils disent nos maisons sous-loués à plus opaque que nous
nos toits devenus piétonniers
et nous autres volailles bondissant tels cailloux sur l'épaule gauche
    de la terre

< 210 >

8.

Brought back to their thickness, the runaways are treated like
    ghosts
entitled to use only the sound of light
the shadow of noise
a door in a drawing

9.

Freshly repainted
the newcomers ask us about what they've left behind
while they ought to let us know what we've become
tell us if we're vague or precise
wet or dry
they laugh to see us so thin while they lose weight each time the
    planet moves
when the top becomes bottom
dragging the horizon and the laundry on clotheslines after it
sheets or shrouds, what's the difference

10.

They say thinkable things which no one remembers
on cracked plates and umbrellas turned inside out by the wind
but they finesse November which closes its doors behind the last
    visitor and on the healthy ones who take over the alleys again

they say our houses are rented out to those who are more opaque
    than we
our roofs are for pedestrians
and we , fowl hopping like pebbles on the earth's left shoulder

< 211 >

11.

Casaniers comme des chevaux farouches comme if surgi d'un
    rocher
nous sursautons lorsqu'un caillou dévale la pente
les bruits à trois dimensions dépassent notre entendement
notre préférence va à l'étale au rectiligne jamais au circulaire
qui nous assiège pour mieux nous surveiller

on nous aborde de biais pour ne pas nous érafler
on nous traite d'insidieux alors que nous sommes inoffensifs et que
    nos murs sont roulés dans les angles tels matelas des pauvres

12.

À l'étroit de nos cages
nous écrivons sans bouger la main
les mots qui nous font défaut pris dans des livres désaffectés

meurs si tu veux disons-nous à celui qui efface son contour
mais nettoie ton espace de tes échardes
meurs pour te réveiller avec ce coq qui clame le jour trois strates
    plus haut

13.

Les passants qui nous empruntent disent nos faces closes sur de
    grandes insatisfactions
ils sont ceux qui parlent
nous sommes ceux qui écoutent
leurs colères brèves comme feu de résineux nous suivent
nous échangeons nos impressions avec des autres obscurcis
    consignés dans les cahiers
marchons sans nous déplacer jambes écartées telle maison bâtie
    sur un fleuve

< 212 >

11.

We are homebodies like wild horses, like a yew growing out of a
     rock
who jump when a pebble rolls down the hill
three-dimensional noises are beyond our understanding
our preference goes to the steady over the rectangular, never to the
     circular
which beseiges us in order to keep better watch on us

they approach us tangentially so as not to scratch us
call us treacherous when we are harmless and have our walls rolled
     up in corners like the mattresses of the poor

12.

In the tight space of our cages
without moving our hands, we write
the words which we lack, taken from disused books

die if you like, we say to the one who erases his outline
but clean your splinters up after you
die to be awakened when the rooster crows three levels above you

13.

The passersby who make use of us say our faces are closed up on
     great dissatisfactions
they are the ones who speak
we, the ones who listen
their rages brief as pine fires follow us
we exchange our impressions with other darkened ones shut up in
     notebooks
walk without moving legs spread like a house built over a river

< 213 >

comment avancer alors que nous avons un pied dans l'eau un pied
    sur la berge
comment nous exprimer alors que nous nous interdisons de mettre
    un nom sur les objets
et que nous prenons une rue de brouette pour un soleil

14.

Une pierre sur la tête
nous ramassons nos ombres pressés d'atteindre la muraille avent
    d'être désuets
le claquement d'un drap sur un corde appelle un lit défait
le bruit d'une bassine est cri d'eau dans un gosier tari
les femmes qui essorent larmes et oreillers nous prennnet pour du
    divet debout sur l'air
ce soir
avant de se couler contre les murs
elles déchiffrent les rayures de nos ongles sur leurs vitres
puis diront
qu'ils hachurent ce qui reflète et s'habite si telle est leur volonté
    mais qu'ils ne touchent pas à un seul cheveu du hêtre

15.

Les essoreuses posent les mêmes questions
pourquoi avez-vous arraché le cheveu blanc de l'if
pourquoi vivez-vous seuls alors que vous pouvez épouser toute
    une forêt
pourquoi les femmes qui vous ouvrent leurs murs vous assignet
    une place entre la hâche et l'âtre et
pourquoi celles qui vous connaissent par ouie dire lisent vos noms
    par temps de neiges et de questionnement?

< 214 >

how to move forward when we have one foot in the water and one
    on the bank
how to express ourselves when we forbid ourselves to give objects
    a name
and mistake a wagon wheel for the sun

14.

With stones on our heads
we gather up our shadows in a hurry to get to the city wall before
    we become outdated
the flap of a sheet on a line recalls an unmade bed
the sound of a bowl is water crying out in a dry throat
the women who wring out tears and pillows take us for goose-
    down standing in the air
this evening
before sliding along the walls
they will decipher the scratches of our nails on their windowpanes
then they'll say
let them scratch what reflects and what lives there at will, but don't
    touch a single hair of the beech tree

15.

The wringers ask the same questions
why have you plucked out the yew tree's one white hair
why do you live alone when you could marry a whole forest
why do the women who open their walls to you give you a place
    between the axe and the hearth and
why do the women who know you by hearsay read your names in
    times of snow and interrogation?

< 215 >

16.

Assises sur le bord des villes
les essoreuses abritent eau et enfants dans leur jarre
leur jardin sous la voûte mauve de leurs aisselles
et dans la hûche leurs morts affamés
les choses étroites qu'elles tricotent ont la patience des laines
tardives et la soumission des troupeaux transis
mais il suffit d'une maille éffilochée pour qu'elles recommencent le
même feu
sans faire la différence entre un pain levé par la lune et un pain cuit
entre deux pierres

Elles disent le basilic exsangue   les morts plein de vigeur
elles disent le basilic incapable d'arrêter la mer
le basilic ne sait pas écrire son nom
ne sait pas qu'il s'appelle basilic

17.

À chaque fin de neige et de boue émiettée
quand les lucarnes se prennent pour des soleils
les essoreuses ramassent les chats qui marchent sur leur corde à
linge
les répartissent entre leurs poches pour les soustraire à l'avidité du
puits
mariage et veuvage les laissent riches d'une maison qu'elles cèdent
volontiers aux passants
ne gardant que la flaque d'eau nécessaite au bain des oiseaux

< 216 >

16.

Seated at the city limits
the wringers shelter water and children in their pitchers
their gardens in their armpits' mauve vault
and the starving dead in the bread box
the narrow things they knit have the patience of late-grown wool
    and the submissiveness of frozen flocks
but all it takes is a dropped stitch for them to begin lighting the
    same fire
not distinguishing between bread the moon makes rise and bread
    baked between two stones

They say the basil is bloodless   and the dead energetic
they say the basil is incapable of stopping the sea
the basil doesn't know how to write its name
doesn't know it's called basil

17.

At the end of every storm of snow and splattered mud
when the skylights take themselves for suns
the wringers collect the cats walking on their clotheslines
stuff them in their many pockets to save them from the wells'
    gluttony
marriage and widowhood endow them with houses they give up
    willingly to passersby
keeping for themselves only the puddle of water they need for the
    birdbath

18.

Les essoreuses n'ouvrent pas à la marée qui fouette leurs murs et
   leur sang à chaque lunaison
ni ne déchiffrent l'écriture rageuse du sel sur leur vitre
l'alphabet translucide n'est que gesticulations d'eau sur la voie
   blanche tracée par la lune un racourci pour les morts des va-nu-
   pieds

le phare fait la sourde oreille quand des jeunes vagues étreignent
   ses genoux
sa responsabilité va aux aînées tirées au cordeau et à un horizon
   capable de basculer du mauvais côté s'il prenait à la terre l'envie
   de se retourner

19.

En haut

plus haut que nos toits
ils honorent le jour de nuit
seuls les morts et les nouveaux mariés sont portés sur les épaules
les femmes d'eau fraîche stagnant dans l'indifférence des puits
le même sillon va du champ au ventre et la même odeur froide de
   silence
alors que leurs filles qui chevauchent la montagne à cru sentent les
   pierres lourdes et les orages qui roulent sur la pente
les livres disent-elles sont les enfants du chagrin
les épluchures des épluchures des forêts
mieux vaut déchiffrer la sueur sur le tambour tendu des reins
et que résonne le galop d'une jument rouge entre les hanches
les filles qui chevauchent la montagne à cru ignorent que les
   mêmes lignes se croisent sur nos boîtes et leur pain
que nous bousculons les ténèbres afin que leur odeur s'infiltre dans
   toutes nos cavités
que pourchassant nos corps nous nous pleurons en elles alors
   qu'elles croient nous pleurer

< 218 >

18.

The wringers don't open their doors to the tide which whips their
    walls and their blood each lunar cycle
they don't decipher the salt's angry handwriting on their panes
its translucent alphabet is only the gesticulations of water on a
    white path scribbled by the moon a shortcut for dead beggars

the lighthouse turns a deaf ear when young waves hug its knees
its responsibilty is to their straight-lined elders and to a horizon
    capable of tipping toward the wrong side if the earth decided to
    turn over

19.

Up there

higher than our roofs
they praise the day at night
only the dead and newlyweds are carried aloft on their shoulders
the freshwater women stagnate in the wells' indifference
the same furrow runs from field to womb with the same cold odor
    of silence
while their daughters who ride the mountain bareback smell the
    heavy stones and storms rolling on the slope
books, they say, are the children of sorrow
the peelings of peelings of the forest
it's better to decipher the sweat on the loins' stretched drum-skin
and let a red mare's galloping resonate between your thighs
the girls who ride the mountain bareback don't know that the
    same lines cross our boxes and their bread
that we shake up the shadows so their odor can seep into all our
    cavities
that pursuing our bodies we mourn for ourselves in them while
    they think they are mourning for us

< 219 >

VÉNUS KHOURY-GHATA is a Lebanese poet and novelist, resident in France since 1973, author of many collections of poems and novels. She received the Prix Mallarmé in 1987 for *Monologue du mort*, the Prix Apollinaire in 1980 for *Les Ombres et leurs cris*, and the Grand Prix de la Société des gens de lettres for *Fables pour un peuple d'argile* in 1992. Her *Anthologie personnelle*, a selection of her previously published and new poems, was published in France by Actes Sud in 1997. Her most recent collection, *Quelle est la nuit parmi les nuits*, was published by Mercure de France in 2004. Her work has been translated into Arabic, Dutch, German, Italian, and Russian, and she was named a Chevalier de la Légion d'Honneur in 2000.

MARILYN HACKER is a winner of the National Book Award in Poetry and the author of eleven books, including *Winter Numbers*, which received a Lambda Literary Award and the Lenore Marshall Poetry Prize in 1995; *Selected Poems*, which was awarded the Poets' Prize in 1996; and the verse novel, *Love, Death, and the Changing of the Seasons*. Her latest collections are *Desesperanto* and *Essays on Departure: New and Selected Poems*. She is a noted translator, most recently of *Charlestown Blues* by Guy Goffette, *Birds and Bison* by Claire Malroux, and *She Says* by Vénus Khoury-Ghata. Hacker lives in New York and Paris and is currently Professor of English at City College. She also teaches Literary Translation at the CUNY Graduate Center.

Nettles was typeset in Dante, a font created by Giovanni Mardersteig in 1957 and originally handcut by Charles Malin. The digital font version was redrawn by Ron Carpenter. Book design by Wendy Holdman. Composition by Prism Publishing Center. Manufactured by Sheridan Books on acid-free paper.